OAKTON COMMUNITY COLLEGE LIBRARY

W9-CBG-309

π

OAKTON COMMUNITY COLLEGE
DES PLAINES CAMPUS
1600 EAST GOLF ROAD
DES PLAINES, IL 60016

PI PRESS
NEW YORK

The Dollhouse Murders

A Forensic Expert Investigates 6 Little Crimes

Thomas P. Mauriello

With Ann Darby

Photographs by John Consoli

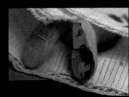

PI PRESS

An Imprint of Pearson Education, Inc.
1185 Avenue of the Americas, New York, New York 10011

© 2004 Pearson Education, Inc.
All rights reserved. No part of this book may be reproduced, in any form or by any means, without permission in writing from the publisher.

Pi Press offers discounts for bulk purchases. For information contact U.S. Corporate and Government Sales, 1-800-382-3419, or corpsales@pearsontechgroup.com. For sales outside the U.S.A., please contact: International Sales, 1-317-581-3793, or international@pearsontechgroup.com.

Company and product names mentioned herein are the trademarks or registered trademarks of their respective owners.

Printed in the United States of America

First Printing

Library of Congress Cataloging-in-Publication Data
A CIP catalog record for this book can be obtained from the Library of Congress.

Pi Press books are listed at www.pipress.net

ISBN 0-13-145165-0

Pearson Education Ltd.
Pearson Education Australia Pty., Limited
Pearson Education Singapore, Pte. Ltd.
Pearson Education North Asia Ltd.
Pearson Education Canada, Ltd.
Pearson Educación de Mexico, S.A. de C.V.
Pearson Education — Japan
Pearson Education Malaysia, Pte. Ltd.

DISCARD

Contents

Preface

"I see no more than you, but I have trained myself to notice what I see."

−Sir Arthur Conan Doyle
The Adventure of the Blanched Soldier

Since 1980, I have taught a course that I designed for the Department of Criminology and Criminal Justice at the University of Maryland at College Park, titled *Introduction to Criminalistics*. Criminalistics, more commonly known as forensic sciences, is the scientific examination of physical evidence so that it can be made most useful in a court of law. Initially most of the students signing up for the class were undergraduate criminal justice and pre-law students, but very soon biology and chemistry majors began enrolling. Many of them were thinking about working in a crime laboratory when they graduated, and indeed, many of them are now doing so.

The course was designed to take a strategic look at the scientific methods used in the investigation, detection, and resolution of criminal activity. As a class, we have explored all the vital phases of the forensic sciences and the criminal investigation process by means of class lectures, audiovisual presentations, crime laboratory exercises, text readings, and the opportunity to learn from visiting forensic scientists who were experts in their respective fields. Although the course was popular with the students—especially with the addition of our crime laboratory on campus—after about ten years, I realized there was something missing. The students' lack of understanding of how to apply the theories they were learning still affected their ability to integrate their newfound knowledge into a practical setting. Academia tends to teach each topic of study separately, and as a result students cannot grasp how each topic depends on others.

In early 1992 I had an insight about how we could improve the situation. I visited the Medical Examiner's Office of the State of Maryland in Baltimore, and while I was there, I came upon a room that had a series of dollhouses displayed in elaborate settings. I learned that an eccentric millionaire who founded Harvard's Department of Legal Medicine, the nation's first university program in forensic pathology, donated a number of her dollhouses to the Medical Examiner's Office. International Harvester heiress Francis Glessner created these miniature one-inch-scale death scene dollhouses in the 1940s and 50s and named them "nutshell studies." She used them in an annual homicide investigation seminar that trained homicide investigators from all over the country. Those seminars are still being hosted today by the state of Maryland some 40 years after her death. This concept appeared to be the answer to my problem. For my class, I decided to create dollhouse dioramas focusing on the crime scene investigation process and demonstrating the importance of a strategic investigation that marshals a variety of professional teams.

I immediately went to work on my "Crime Scene Cases." The University of Maryland's Department of Criminology and Criminal Justice commissioned Nathaniel "Doc" Hodgdon of

Doctor's Dollhouse of Severna Park, Maryland, to design and construct the dioramas. Doc, his wife, and daughter built the dioramas with Plexiglas ceilings and front walls. Doc's assistant, Sherry Zadow, did the interior design. Each diorama is a one-inch-scale, miniaturized crime scene, representing an exact replica of how a crime scene would appear according to the scenario I wrote.

Doctor's Dollhouse worked closely with me to ensure that each diorama was constructed to provide a realistic setting, consistent with each pre-written scenario. The final stages called for the assistance of two of my criminal justice students, Frank Mort and John Shoemaker, who helped me with the final crime scene scenario development and selection of specific physical evidence exhibits to be left at each crime scene consistent with the scenarios. I created the physical evidence representations with the assistance of graphic artists Arthur Green and Pamela Shaffer; sculpture artist Candace Beck; and decorative artist, my lovely wife, Laurie Mauriello. All the physical evidence is simulated in each scene except for latent fingerprints. At a one-inch scale, it would be impossible to see fingerprint ridge details; therefore, they are not present in the scenes.

The dioramas were first used in my class during the fall semester of the same year, 1992. They have been in use as a teaching aid ever since, and have proven to be an excellent method of testing students' specific knowledge of the crime scene investigation process and physical evidence recognition. During the laboratory exercise, the students conduct a crime scene investigation, and in doing so they must examine the crime scene, identify all the evidence, and ask the right questions of victims and witnesses.

Watching crime dramas on television is a passive experience. My students must place themselves in the mindsets of ordinary characters and crime scene professionals. Because the crime scene is the first stage of the investigation, crime laboratory results are not available, but nevertheless, the process begins—either on the right track or the wrong one. Uniformed police officers are usually the first responders representing the legal process. They take the initial report, determine what crime has been committed, and then turn it over to the detectives if it is determined to be a felony. Meanwhile, EMTs (emergency medical technicians) arrive to render medical assistance to injured victims.

And then there are the detectives, who are responsible for conducting and managing the investigation of felony cases. Under their management, the evidence technicians (on the West Coast they are referred to as the criminalists) process the crime scene by searching, photographing and sketching the crime scene then finding, identifying, collecting, packaging, and transporting all physical evidence to the crime laboratory. Finally, there is the medical examiner, who is responsible for examining a body at a crime scene and subsequently autopsying the body to determine the manner, mode, time, and cause of death.

Forensic science as depicted on television can give the impression that everything done in an investigation—from responding to the crime scene and identifying and examining evidence to interviewing witnesses and arresting suspects—is done by one group of players, who happen to be the stars of the television show. This is an unrealistic view of a process that requires many different teams and kinds of professionals. Of course one of the most important is the first detective on the scene, the person who sets in motion a strategic investigation. And it is this character who is at the beginning, middle, and end of the narrative versions of the dioramas that have been written for this book.

Following the detective in these pages—no particular detective, no particular doll, just an off-camera guy doing his job—and looking at what he looks at will enable readers to get a better idea of how modern crime investigation really occurs. In these simple stories, the fundamental questions of all serious crime scenes are set out. And their dollhouse resolution is often, like human justice, only the best we can do.

I would like to acknowledge the vision of Stephen Morrow who recognized that readers would be interested in the realities of true crime scene investigation; Ann Darby, a brilliant writer who was able to take my technical writing, thoughts, and ideas and transpose them into storylines that capture the theory and practice of the crime scene investigation process; John Consoli, the photographer on this project who captured a sense of realism and brought the dollhouses to life; and Juliet Turner, editor, Matthew Bender & Company, Inc., publisher of my legal textbook, Criminal Investigation Handbook. Finally, I acknowledge Dr. Charles F. Wellford, the Chair of the Department of Criminology and Criminal Justice, who was willing to fund the dollhouse initiative when I first approached him with the idea. This exemplifies Dr. Wellford's dedication to the criminal justice sciences and our students at the University of Maryland, which has made our Department a nationally recognized center of academic excellence.

–T.P.M.

The camera flashed repeatedly in the dimness as the evidence technician walked slowly around the living room at 6903 Pleasant Street, stopping every few inches to snap a shot or two of another piece of evidence. And there was a lot of evidence at this crime scene: abandoned tools, abandoned loot, opened doors, and blood. Grim though it was, that pleased the Detective. The tech had just shot the tools of the burglar's trade, the crowbar, bolt cutters, and flashlight, which lay near the front door. She was now shooting the nearby bloodstain in the pale gold carpet, and it was the blood that the Detective was studying. He stood between the victim, an older white male who lay in his pajamas on the floor, and a table lamp—a Tiffany table lamp—that was smashed on the wall-to-wall. The Detective was particularly interested in how clean the carpet was beneath his feet. He crouched and studied the nap, yet for all his looking, he found no blood around him—none at all. There was a trail of blood leading from the front door to the china cabinet to the shattered lamp on the Detective's right. And to the Detective's left, the victim lay in a puddle of blood, for he had bled copiously from the head. But, in the expanse between the victim and the lamp, there was nothing.

Which the Detective wanted to discuss with his partner. He wanted to say, "That trail of blood there? It's not our victim's. It's the assailant's." But his partner seemed distracted this morning. He slowly rubbed the back of his head and stared out the window—toward the street where the squad cars and the mobile crime laboratory waited and the uniformed officers kept the crime scene secure and the neighbors at bay.

What the Detective did say was, "We've got one dead man alone in a house. And we've got a roomful of evidence. This room is talking to us, buddy. It would talk a lot faster if you pitched in."

His partner—a stocky, blunt-featured man who liked to follow his instincts—wheeled toward him. "I want to interview the kid again."

"Following your instincts, are you?"

The Detective thought instinct was another word for appetite, and in his experience, following your appetites only got you in trouble. So he took his time answering his partner, as he did whenever he disagreed with him. The camera flashed twice more, and the Detective watched the evidence tech get two more shots—one of the coffee table pushed back against the sofa and one of the newspaper the boy must have dropped—before peering out the window himself. On the sidewalk, the boy's squat bike leaned into its kickstand, and his sack of papers slumped against a sweet gum tree, at least half a route not delivered. The boy himself seemed to be in the charge of a uniformed officer, who, the Detective could see, was casting idle talk in the boy's direction. But even from this distance, it was clear the boy didn't want to talk. The Detective wouldn't want to either, not if he was 11 again and had just seen his first stiff. The uniformed officer said they would call the boy's parents. But no woman rushed from her morning routine had arrived yet; no man either. No one who resembled the boy had come to claim him. He'd given his name as Jimmy Price, but he looked middle-something: Middle Eastern or Central American—with small, fine features and dark eyes. The boy must have felt the Detective staring, for he gazed back at him, his expression both sad and wary.

"You think he can tell us anything more than he did 10 minutes ago?"

"We've seen boys a lot younger commit crimes a lot worse."

"We have," the Detective agreed. "But when was the last time one of them called 911 and waited for us on the sidewalk outside the crime scene?"

The boy had been sitting under the tree, next to his newspapers, when their car pulled up at 7:05 a.m. He'd waited better than half an hour, apparently doing nothing more than twisting a rubber band around his fingers.

"Humor me," his partner said.

"Don't I always?"

The evidence tech had progressed across the room. She was photographing the blood around the lamp, the blood on the shattered amber lampshade. The Detective noted the blood on the shards of stained glass and turned to gaze again at the victim, a Mr. Floyd Henderson, according to the uniformed officers who had first responded to the 911 call. They were the ones who had made sure there were no other victims in the house, and no assailants. They were the ones who had eyeballed all the rooms, noting as they did that the victim's bed was rumpled and unmade, as if he'd slept in it at least part of the night. They were the ones who had spotted the billfold atop the victim's dresser and gingerly flipped it open to see the driver's license in the ID window. Floyd M. Henderson, according to the license, date of birth, November 7, 1936.

The man lay on his back by the open door. The wound to his right temple was deep, deep enough to kill a man, the Detective thought. By this time, the surface of the blood pooled on the carpet had congealed. Because of the bloody lampshade, the Detective was tempted to conclude the assailant had struck the victim with the lamp when he entered the room. The door opened to the right, if one entered from the hall, the lamp lay to the door's right, and the wound was to the victim's right temple. Odd thing was, the victim lay on his back, not his stomach. Someone strikes you as you enter a room and you fall forward, you fall on your face, don't you? Could someone have struck the victim as he tried to leave the room? Was there more than one assailant? This raised enough doubt; the Detective gave up his objections to requestioning the boy. "Just don't bring him in this house," the Detective said to his partner. "We've got a clean scene here, and I mean to keep it that way."

"Every day you sound more like my mother."

"Maybe if you'd listened to her…"

"You know, it wouldn't hurt to scare the boy."

The Detective shook his head, but again took his time. He slid a hand into a latex glove, then knelt and lifted the lamp, using the cord to avoid disturbing latent prints. "Brass," he said. "Pretty damn heavy for an 11-year-old to wield. And our victim's not short, you know."

"You think he was struck with the lamp?" the partner asked.

"I can't say. The wound to the head's deep—a skull cracker. Think a Tiffany lampshade could do that?" To the evidence tech, the Detective said, "Be sure to look for glass around the victim, okay?"

She nodded. "You noticed the blood on the base, right?"

"Ah," he said, noting a crescent of blood, like maroon lacquer, on the base. "I'm noticing it now." The Detective swiveled toward his partner. "I think this guy's been cold for hours, buddy, and how do you know it wouldn't hurt to scare the boy?"

"I'm telling you, he knows something. He acts like he knows."

"All right, all right," the Detective said, following his partner, and then, only half-joking, added, "Hey! Don't track through the blood."

The Detective and his partner didn't want to interview the boy anywhere near the crowd of prying neighbors, so they waved him over, and he headed reluctantly across the lawn, then veered to the brick path, as if he'd been taught not to walk on the grass. Though it wasn't yet 7:30 a.m., it was mid-July and already muggy, the way summers can be. It seemed more so now they were outside, and the Detective realized the victim had central air—nice, quiet central air that let him keep the windows closed in summer. Which led the Detective to glance toward the front window, observing for the first time it was in fact closed.

"I want to go over this again," his partner was saying to the boy. "You were delivering papers on your regular route, and you reached this house at what time?"

"At 6:30. I told you."

"You did, didn't you?" the partner said, too innocently. "But you know something? I don't see a watch on your wrist."

"I told you. I saw the clock on the table by the phone."

"That's after you walked into the house, right?"

"Yes," the boy said wearily.

"So tell me again why you walked into Mr. Henderson's house."

"I brought the paper to the door…"

"You always deliver his paper to the door?"

"Yes, because he's old."

Each time he answered, the boy gazed directly at the Detective's partner, afterwards averting his gaze, but not his face. He gave the impression of both obedience and evasion. You can look but you can't see me. The boy possessed a private patience, the Detective decided, like a bookish child, or a child used to playing alone, or a child accustomed to waiting without complaint until the adults showed up—a latchkey child, perhaps.

The boy brightened and said, "I deliver the paper to the door for all the old people."

"Yeah, yeah," the partner said. "I used to do that, too. For the tips."

"For tips?" The boy looked puzzled. "I do it because it's hard for Papi…"

The partner interrupted, "So the door was closed when you brought the paper?"

"No, I told you. It was open…" The boy held his hands a few inches apart. "Just a little, like Mr. Henderson had forgotten to close it, and where the lock-thing goes looked broken and the chain was broken…"

"You saw the chain?" the partner asked. "The chain inside the door?"

"Yes, I looked for it. I told you."

"So what did you do?"

"I called out, 'Mr. Henderson? Mr. Henderson, you okay?'" The boy paused. "When he didn't answer, I pushed open the door and saw him lying on the floor, and he didn't look right."

"You see anything else?"

"I saw Mr. Henderson, that's all, and I thought he was dead, so I walked in and picked up the phone and called the number, 911."

"You ever been in Mr. Henderson's house before?"

"No, except when he paid me. I'd go in and he'd pay me, and I'd go out."

"But, you knew where the phone was?"

"It was right in front of me, right on the table."

"And you didn't see the blood everywhere? You didn't see the pillowcase?"

"I saw Mr. Henderson, and I called because I thought he might be dead."

A car passed slowly—a neighbor rubbernecking the black-and-whites, the Detective thought—and the boy turned around, plainly disappointed when he didn't recognize the driver.

He said, "After I called, I saw he was bleeding. It was only 6:30, and the lights weren't on. It was gray in there."

"So it was dark?" the partner asked. "And you could still see Mr. Henderson? You could see the telephone?"

"It wasn't dark. It was gray," the boy answered. "I could see the phone and Mr. Henderson. They're light."

This the partner couldn't deny: The phone was yellow; Mr. Henderson had white hair and fair skin. "Did you say 'was bleeding'? Did you mean he was still bleeding when you saw him?"

"Come on, buddy. That's enough." The Detective patted his partner's shoulder. "Jimmy doesn't know. I wouldn't know; you wouldn't know. But let me ask, Jimmy." The Detective took a few steps back, because he was tall and didn't want to loom over the boy. "Did you touch anything or move anything inside the house?"

"The phone. I touched the phone."

"But you didn't move the table? Or the coffee table? You didn't try to help Mr. Henderson?"

At this the boy did look away. "No, I didn't help him. I was scared."

The Detective sighed. "Yeah, well, we're all scared, Jimmy."

"But listen, Jimmy," the partner said, "did you ever tell anyone else about the nice things you saw in Mr. Henderson's house?"

"What nice things?"

The Detective intervened, "Wedgwood, Waterford, Poole. Those words don't mean anything to you, do they?"

The boy shook his head.

"I didn't think so." To his partner, the Detective said, "You go study the rosebushes, buddy. I'm going to walk our witness over to those officers and make sure they take good care of him."

"What rosebushes?" his partner asked.

"Turn around. You'll see. And while you're at it, think how nice it would be to have central air."

"Central air?"

"Exactly."

As they walked, the Detective told the boy he was sorry some of his customers might complain, just because he'd done the right thing. "Sometimes it happens that way." He scanned the neighbors in their robes and Bermuda shorts and running clothes, making sure no nosy Parker was looking their way. "Could you do one thing for me, Jimmy? Could you show me your hands?"

The boy held them out, and the Detective examined first the palms and then the backs of his hands, especially the fingernails. He found newsprint and little-boy dirt, but no residue of blood, nothing to suggest a struggle. Before he passed the boy along to the uniformed officer, he said, "They're going to need your fingerprints, so we can tell your prints from the bad guy's prints. You understand that?" The Detective waited for the boy to nod, then added, "So I want you to give the officers your mother's work number, okay?" The boy wouldn't answer, so the Detective added, "She clocks in early, just like my partner and me, doesn't she? I promise you, her boss will let her come get you. My boss would." The boy held his gaze, then slanted his eyes away. A camera flashed, and from the crowd, a guy in a pork pie hat and retro baggy trousers called out a question. Such a shame he couldn't hear it, the Detective thought.

The medical examiner pulled her car in across the street. The uniformed officers told the bystanders to stand back and, when the ME passed through, lifted the CRIME SCENE tape so she could step under it. Although not as tall as the Detective, the ME was tall, and everything about her suggested physical and mental competence. (He'd never play one-on-one with her, that was for sure, not unless he wanted to lose.) While the Detective told her what he'd surmised as they approached the house—a 67-year-old white male had interrupted a burglary and taken a blow to the head—the ME speed-dialed her cell phone.

To the phone she said, "We've got a pickup at 6903 Pleasant Street. Going to the morgue, per usual." To the Detective, she said, "That was the funeral home we use for transport. Give me a few minutes to photograph the body and do my prelim. Then we'll talk."

Standing on the front path, the evidence tech was sketching in her notebook, drawing a rough plan of the entire house. The Detective's partner crouched on the edge between the lawn and the flowerbed that bordered the house. The tulips and irises had wilted away, but the rosebushes were still blooming and had recently been watered.

"Central air?" the partner said when the Detective approached him. "So you're saying that window there is locked? You're saying our murderer tried the window first, then walked over to the front steps, leaving those footprints for us? Well, what do you know?"

"Fact is, I don't know if it's locked. I'd bet money it is."

"I'd say that's a men's size 11." The partner pointed at the prints. "Deep enough, aren't they? Nice that he didn't get clever and walk on the grass."

Walking on the grass themselves, they joined the evidence tech. The Detective said, "We've got footprints over here."

"We do," the tech said. "And I think we've got spatter here on the brick steps, and over there on the neighbor's drive-way." She indicated a Pollock-like arc of dark brown spots on the concrete drive. "Plus here on the doorjamb and on the inside doorknob, that's got to be blood. I can run a field test for you, just to confirm these spots here are blood." Quickly, she reviewed her plans with the detectives: the blood samples she intended to take, the evidence she would box or bag, and the order in which she would do all this. Dusting for prints she would save for last, lest the dust contaminate the other evidence. Now she added "benzidine color test," "footprints," and "soil sample" to her list.

"Would be so nice if we found a suspect with Mr. Henderson's soil on his shoe," the partner said.

The Detective and his partner then re-examined the front door and jamb they'd studied only briefly when they arrived. The door had been pried from the doorjamb, deep tool marks pressed into the wood. In the process, the catch for the lock had been broken and also forced from the jamb.

"We hold that crowbar up here, bet it matches these tool marks exactly," the partner said. "Ditto the bolt cutter and the chain."

"Let's make sure the tech gets photos of the striations the tools made and silicone rubber casts of the door and jamb," the Detective said, "so we've got proof the crowbar was used to force the door."

"Right," the partner said.

They stepped inside the house, and the ME glanced up but did not interrupt her work. "Let's try the window," the Detective said, and his partner slipped on his latex gloves, then lifted the curtain and tried the window. "Locked, just like you said."

"Our burglar must have pressed hard on the frame out-side," the Detective said. "We should have some very clear prints out there. Let's make sure the tech gets them."

"All right. Our guy can't open the window, so he forces the door open and cuts the chain, comes in and pulls out his flashlight," the partner said. "Then what? He just drops his tools on the floor?"

"I think he comes in and sets up shop, makes himself comfortable," the Detective said. "He turns on his flashlight and makes a work area for himself on the area rug." The Detective knelt and ran his fingers over the depressions in the carpet that marked the usual position of the coffee table. "He push-es this table out of his way, maybe even moves the telephone table." The Detective skimmed his fingers over the carpet until he found the dents from the occasional table. "Yeah, he did!"

"I'm surprised he didn't make a ham sandwich and pour himself a glass of milk."

"Maybe he did," the Detective said. "Take another look. And while you're in there, make sure our burglar didn't take anything else."

His partner gone, the Detective studied the tools again. They looked heavy, heavier than the tools the Detective car-ried for his job. Had the burglar worn a tool belt? Or carried a pack? Or stashed the tools in the inner pockets of a coat, a coat large enough to conceal a crowbar and bolt cutters—that would stand out on a hot summer night. The flashlight was switched to OFF, a piece of evidence that confirmed a bit of Jimmy Price's story: No lights were on when he walked in.

"Don't want to interrupt," the ME said. She had just finished covering the victim's hands with paper bags to protect poten-tial traces of evidence—blood, skin, or chemical residues. "But I can give you my prelim."

The Detective knew what she was looking for. He knew that once the heart stopped pumping, blood succumbed to gravity, seeking its lowest level, and muscle cells slowly starved, burning up their fuel and excreting lactic acid, mak-ing the muscles tight. The gradual stiffening of the body and settling of the blood would tell the ME roughly when the vic-tim died. The pooling of the blood wherever the body touched the floor—the pressure points—would tell her if the victim had been moved.

"Here's what I can say so far. Judging by post-mortem rigor mortis and lividity, the victim died six or seven hours ago. I'd place the approximate time of death at 1:00 a.m. The pres-sure points are consistent with the victim's present position.

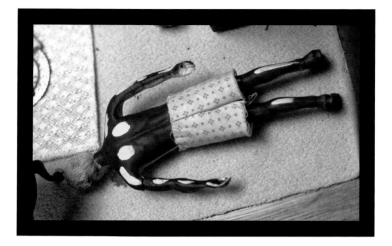

I'd say he died where he's lying. Outside the lab, I can't say much about the blow to his head, but it is a gouge. The tech should handle that brass lamp carefully. I wouldn't be surprised if the base of the lamp matches the impression in his skull."

"The lamp," the Detective said, his whole body swaying in agreement, "the base of it."

He gazed at the ME pointedly, as if he'd just asked her a serious question. She answered, "No, I don't see any sign of struggle. But I've got nothing more to say, Detective, not until the pathologist has done her autopsy." The ME flipped open her cell phone and speed-dialed again. "Hugo? Hugo?" she said after a moment. "Where are your guys? This body needs to go."

While the ME waited for body transport, the evidence technician returned and began collecting blood samples around the room. Blood that was still wet she drew into a fine pipette and dropped into a vial. Dry blood she scraped with an X-Acto knife onto a clean sheet of paper she carefully folded. The Detective stepped out of the way and stared down at the sack—the pillowcase—of loot the burglar had left behind.

A lightweight pillowcase, easy to fold and stow, but large enough to hold several pieces of valuable silver, crystal, and china. The burglar had made good progress. The pillowcase was well-stuffed, and the china cabinet was all but empty— only a large tureen and a German beer stein left behind. A pewter chalice lay overturned on the floor, perhaps the last piece the burglar had planned to pack.

"If our guy ate something, he left no signs. But I'll tell you," his partner said bluffly as he returned to the room. "Mr. Henderson's got a Sub-Zero and Cuisinart appliances everywhere—you know, the chopper thing? But he's also got a toaster and a coffeemaker. And he's got one of those mini TVs, right on the counter."

"And not one of them lifted," the Detective replied in a quieter voice.

"Looks that way. And not the TV in the bedroom, either."

"Cash and credit cards still in Mr. Henderson's billfold," the Detective said. "Didn't even go for them after the victim was dead."

"So the guy knows exactly what he wants," the partner said. "He's got a fancy fence for fine silver and china. He doesn't mess with mass-consumer products."

"But does he know where what he wants is?" the Detective asked. "Exactly where?"

"My point about Jimmy Price, Detective First-Class."

The Detective bridled to hear his senior rank bandied, but he moved ahead. "Could be the victim had some workmen in the house recently. Hired someone to move some furniture or clean the carpets—someone who had a chance to scope out the cabinet."

"Why are we so sure it's only one burglar?" the partner asked.

"Good question," the Detective answered. "We're not, and we're not going to be until we have the prints and the blood and the DNA sorted out."

"Looks like our guy packed carefully," the partner said, and nodded toward the pillowcase.

"He was more or less professional," the Detective said, "bringing the tools he needed to burgle: Get in, get the stuff, get out. He wasn't expecting to get caught. He wasn't expecting to murder someone."

"You think Floyd heard our guy and came out to see what was going on?"

"If so, what's the noisiest thing the burglar did?" the Detective asked. "What did Mr. Henderson hear?"

"Breaking and entering's the noisy part."

"That's what I'm thinking. But Mr. Henderson didn't come out until our burglar was all packed up? What was he doing? Lying awake listening?"

"What do you think? He's going to dash out, all Dudley Do-Right, and challenge our guy?"

"But that's my point," the Detective said. "After listening to his burglar, Mr. Henderson gets up, steps into his slippers, and walks to his living room. But he doesn't grab something to protect himself?"

"So maybe he was expecting someone. Maybe he slept through the B & E, then heard some noise in the living room— that pewter thing hitting the shelf, maybe—and walked down the hall saying, 'Honey, is that you?' or whatever." The partner charged ahead, so the Detective knew his partner was operating on instinct again, "Or maybe Floyd didn't hear anything. Maybe Floyd's a little deaf. What's the first thing you do when you wake up in the middle of the night?"

"You know damn well," the Detective said.

"Right, I do. So he flushes and heads to the kitchen, where the water's cold or he can grab a snack or a nip or whatever. He doesn't turn on the lights because who does when they're walking through their own house in the middle of the night?"

"So even if our burglar isn't alert, he hears Mr. Henderson."

The Detective hated to admit his partner had good instincts. "He steps behind the door."

"If I were him," the partner said, "I would have grabbed the crowbar. Pack it in, pack it out, leave no weapon behind. Either our guy doesn't think of it, or he hopes hiding will save him."

"Mr. Henderson opens the door and walks in…"

"Maybe swears or something because he sees the table's moved, the cabinet's open, the sack of stuff on the floor," the partner interjected.

"Our burglar strikes Mr. Henderson on the side of the head." The Detective swung his arm. "The downward blow of the base sent the glass shade up, so it smashed against him— against his arm, most likely."

They heard a rap on the door and turned toward a shoelace of a guy—lanky, long-haired, and so loose-limbed he could have been boneless. Behind him, the corner of a gurney was visible, as was his sidekick. The shoelace said, "Medical examiner called?"

"That's me," the ME said. "You're from the funeral home?" As she oversaw the transport, the Detective and his partner continued to talk. But, when the shoelace of a guy and his sidekick removed the victim's body, they stood quietly, as did the evidence tech, who was working on the blood spilled on the area rug. As soon as the victim and ME were gone, they all resumed their work.

"Here's what I've been wanting to tell you, buddy," the Detective said. "We won't know until the blood's typed, but I think we've got two separate bleeders. The victim, who didn't bleed onto his clothes, who only bled lying down, and the assailant, who cut himself on the lamp and bled all the way out the door."

The partner nodded. "Like he stands there bleeding a moment, then he decides he'd better go?"

"Right. He takes a step or two toward the window," the Detective said, "to see if anyone's watching, leaving those small spots since the blood's just beginning to drip off his arm. Then he comes back to the rug to get the property he came for, bleeding pretty heavily onto that rug. Decides he can't bother with the goods and bolts for the door, pauses again to open the door and make sure no one outside can see him. Leaves his blood on the carpet by the door and on the doorknob and on the jamb. Blood must have been dripping down his arm onto his hand by then."

"That's if all that blood matches," the partner said.

"If it matches," the Detective agreed, then turned to where the victim had been. "Here's what I don't understand. You have any idea, my intuitive friend, how Mr. Henderson ended up on his back?"

"Our guy rolled him over, to see if he was dead?" The partner got down on his hands and knees to scrutinize the carpet. "Or maybe our guy hit Floyd so hard, he spun as he fell."

"Or Mr. Henderson turned to get away," the Detective said, "and then he fell. Maybe an accomplice standing on the other side of the door hit him. Or maybe the blow didn't kill him, but the fall did. We're going to need that autopsy report."

"Cripes!" his partner said, and the Detective smiled privately: If nothing else, he'd trained his partner not to swear in front of him. "I got glass in my hand from the blasted lamp." The partner pulled off his latex glove and sucked the small cut on his palm.

"Watch it," the Detective said.

The evidence tech looked up, alarmed. "Don't you dare drip on our scene and ruin the blood evidence—not after all the work I've done."

The autopsy and blood typing would be complete by the end of the day, while the results of DNA fingerprinting wouldn't be available for weeks. The autopsy would reveal whether Mr. Floyd Henderson died from the blow to his head or from something else. Serology would either confirm or refute the tale the Detective believed the blood told. If their burglar had prior felony convictions and was in the system, the DNA analysis could help the Detective and his partner identify a suspect. Likewise, if the murderer had been arrested and printed before, AFIS—the Automated Fingerprint Identification System—might find a match and a suspect. But for all of that, they had to wait. What the neighbors knew, they could begin to glean immediately.

The Detective and his partner joined the uniformed officers in the street. The boy and his bike and papers were gone, as was one squad car. When asked, a uniformed officer told the Detective the boy's mother had arrived, and she'd gone with him to the station so he could be fingerprinted. The Detective nodded, hating that the boy had to be printed, then scanned the crowd, which had changed, as crowds do with time. The first to arrive, in their robes or jogging clothes, were quiet in their curiosity. By the time the ME arrived, there were more people, more brightly and severely dressed. They seemed both impatient and eager, as if they knew the body would soon be removed. They had to know, the Detective thought, the body would be bagged and they'd see nothing. Yet they waited, trying to brush up against a tragedy that wasn't theirs. Now that the body was gone, only the stragglers remained, the few who happened on the crime scene late and those who needed something other than TV to watch. Among these was a trim, gray-haired woman in a cardigan and pressed slacks. Retired, widowed, or both, she seemed particularly interested, and the Detective made a note to interview her first.

The Detective and his partner decided to work separately; with luck, they could interview the neighbors and prospective witnesses in half the time. The Detective wanted to know the usual: Who had last seen Mr. Henderson, where, and when, and did anyone see or hear anything unusual last night? He also wanted a fix on the victim's social life. Everything in the house said Mr. Henderson lived alone, but was he divorced or a widower? Did he have girlfriends or boyfriends or no friends? Did he have children and did they visit often? And the Detective wanted to interview the neighbors on their property. He wanted permission to look around their front windows and flowerbeds.

"So we're convinced this was an interrupted burglary?" the partner said. "And you want to know if the burglar cased other houses?"

The Detective smiled gently. "Burglars prefer easy targets, unless they're looking for something specific in a specific location. I want to know why our burglar didn't give up when he found the window locked."

"Got it," the partner said, and the two of them moved through the scattering of bystanders, the Detective making his way toward the quiet, gray-haired woman, who turned out to be Mrs. Vivian Ludwig, Mr. Henderson's eastward neighbor. She cooperated, allowing herself to be interviewed and allowing the Detective to examine her front window and the hydrangea bed below it. The neighbor just east of Mrs. Ludwig wasn't home, but the neighbors on the south side of the street were, and by the time the Detective met his partner back at the squad car, he had determined the neighborhood consensus about Mr. Henderson: a very nice, very quiet man with a very green thumb.

Which is what he told his partner as they leaned against the black-and-white in the shade of the sweet gum tree.

"Of the three neighbors I interviewed," the Detective said, "the only one who saw him was Mrs. Ludwig, Vivian Ludwig. She saw him last night, at 8:15 p.m. He was watering his roses, and she dropped over for gardening advice. Anyone you talk to see him?"

"Nope. None of the adults, anyway," the partner said. "Kids were out on their bikes and playing tag, but they didn't notice him."

"Mrs. Ludwig did talk to him, but she said he didn't mention any visitors or guests coming. She knew of no boyfriends or girlfriends and seemed dismayed that I asked."

"My guys all said he was a widower—so, so sad."

The Detective added, "Mrs. Ludwig said his was a messy widowerhood. His second wife, the younger wife, was divorcing him. She was 50-some, but she had a stroke before the papers were signed."

"Ouch!" the partner said.

"She said he had one son, one daughter," the Detective said. "They didn't grow up here, as this is the second home for the second wife. So, she didn't have much to say about them. The others didn't either." He looked back at the single-family house, with its rosebushes and brick walk, its oval window in the front door. The evidence tech came out, picked her way through the rosebushes, and crouched down to take casts of the footprints beneath the window. She must have finished bagging and tagging evidence. Soon she would move on to dusting the immobile pieces for prints: the china cabinet, the doors and door frames, the windows. "Any of your people see a stranger in the neighborhood? Anyone see anyone enter the house? Anyone hear anything?"

"No to all three," the partner said. "They all said it's a quiet, quiet neighborhood. No one could be more surprised."

"And footprints?"

"None at those three houses," the partner said. "I even tried the front windows. Two were unlocked.

"But here's the kicker," the partner continued. The Detective could see the man was pleased with himself. A dimple sliced one broad cheek, and his eyes crinkled. "Mr. Henderson got rid of some furniture last week. These people to the west and this couple across the street seemed to think it was the deceased wife's. Last Saturday, two men in a van carried several pieces away."

"But they don't know who?"

"Green truck. That's all they remembered."

When the autopsy report reached the Detective's inbox, his partner was out of the office on leave (four days in the Smoky Mountains). The Detective read it amid the other papers in his box: a memo about overtime, a toxicology report on a suicide case he'd closed the week before, an information request from Narcotics. The blow to the temple was the cause of death, according to the ME's report, though there was secondary trauma to the brain and skull, attributable to the victim's fall. Close-up photographs of the wound and the base of the table lamp corroborated the hypothesis that the lamp was the murder weapon. There were no other signs of trauma to the body. The lividity, which was fixed, and the rigor mortis were consistent with an approximate time of death of 12:00 a.m. The stomach contents suggested the victim had taken his last meal at roughly 9:00 p.m. The toxicology report was pending. The victim was an otherwise healthy male with atherosclerosis typical of a 60-year-old male.

 The serology report, which appeared in his inbox later in the day, showed only two blood types on the scene: the victim's AB- and the perpetrator's O+. Why couldn't the murderer at least have a rare blood type? The samples were clean—none of the blood got mixed up—and that was good. The report also showed the victim bled where he fell while the murderer bled all over, and that satisfied the Detective. He could pretty much say events transpired the way he thought they had transpired.

Once the fingerprints were sorted—Jimmy Price's and Mr. Henderson's prints identified and separated from the murderer's—there was good news and bad. The good was that the burglar cum murderer left prints everywhere—on the china cabinet, the coffee table, the occasional table, the lamp table, and most tellingly, on the Tiffany table lamp—and many of them were especially clear, such as those on the exterior window frame. The bad news was AFIS couldn't find a match. It was bad luck the murderer hadn't been arrested before. Still, the Detective took a tiny bit of pleasure when he read the print report. It listed the paperboy as Jamie Price, not Jimmy. At least he'd read some tiny part of the story right. He'd puzzled together the hardships of one character. He noticed one oddity in the print report. In the list of evidence printed, he noticed the victim's prints were found on the doorknob to the hallway, but not on the doorknob from the hallway. He discussed it with his partner when he returned, a topic to pass the time as they waited in a courthouse hallway to give testimony in another case.

"Like he always pulled the door open going to the bedroom, but never pulled it closed behind him, and never used it to push the door open coming from the bedroom."

"Some doors you pull with your hand on one side and shove with your shoulder on the other," the partner said.

"You push the handle sometimes, don't you?"

"There's always some fact you can't reconcile, isn't there?" the partner said.

"Getting wise in your old age, buddy."

The forensic lab sent its report on the DNA fingerprinting some two weeks later, and that too was disappointing, for they had found no match for the DNA derived from the murderer's blood. Whoever murdered Mr. Henderson hadn't been tested, perhaps because the burglar had never been arrested, perhaps because he (or maybe she) had never been arrested for a crime that warranted DNA testing, or perhaps because when he or she was last arrested, no one tested DNA.

The Detective's partner returned to 6903 Pleasant Street— where the house and yard were still draped with CRIME SCENE tape—and searched for Mr. Henderson's household receipts and checkbook. He found no check drawn to a mover of any kind and no receipt for any move.

"The guy must have paid cash," he told the Detective. "But I'm obsessed with green vans."

"I know," the Detective said. "So am I. Have been since the day we investigated."

"I've seen Green Belt Movers, Boyz N the Van, Mossy Thumb Nursery, and I don't know how many private vans."

Though the partner checked the records at all three companies, none had picked up furniture on Pleasant Street during the first two weeks of July. When he struck out again with a walk through the Yellow Pages, calling every mover listed, he returned to Green Belt, Boyz, and Mossy to ask about the entire month of June. But he found nada, nothing, nichts.

The Detective and his partner worked other cases, returning to this one to interview the neighbors again and to speak to the son and daughter, who wanted to know how their father died. The case slipped from the A list to the C, though the Detective asked his partner to do one thing: track other suburban burglaries, other breaking and entering cases, on the off chance they would recognize a pattern. It was two months before a similar burglary occurred: In mid-September, a senior

law partner and his wife returned from London to find someone had burglarized their dining room and their dining room
alone. Ten days later, two men who had just moved into a gar-
den condo were burglarized while they were out to dinner:
One of them lost all his mother's silver. In this case, the burglar urinated in the bath, and left very clean prints on the tiles
and the mirror. Shipping manifests led one investigation to an
independent trucker driving for Mayflower. A fence led the
other investigation to a day worker the trucker hired, a
Manfred C. Ocean. Tall, gray, ponytailed, skinny as an old-
time speedballer, with an elaborate tattoo on his shoulder and
back that made the Detective think famed cartoonist R. Crumb
should sue for copyright infringement, he was better known
as Manny Olson.

The prints on the tiles and mirror tied the Henderson case
to the other two. When the District Attorney worked out the
trial schedule, she decided to try the Henderson case first—
not because she wanted the murder conviction, though she
did. But because, she said, she had the cleanest evidence for
that case. It was the surest conviction.

2. The Garage

Attracted by the lights of the vehicles that had descended on this quiet suburban neighborhood—the squad cars, the ME's car, the mobile crime laboratory, and the EMS vehicle, which was just departing—the neighbors had gathered on the sidewalk. The Detective excused himself and slipped past them, heading up the driveway. A dark blue sedan, a family car, was parked in the drive, its door ajar, the warning bell ringing over and over. It must belong to the husband of the victim, the Detective thought, but he passed it by, aiming straight for the garage where the uniformed officer had told him the victim lay.

Like the other garages on the block, this one was attached to a single-story, ranch-style home. Unlike the others, this garage was wrapped with yellow CRIME SCENE tape. Unlike the others, a uniformed officer, a young woman, stood in front of it protectively, warding off anyone who might contaminate the scene. The garage door was up, perhaps left that way by the husband when he found his wife's body, and the Detective could see the victim, or part of her. She lay on the concrete floor, her shod feet extending from a long pink and white skirt. A two-door Ford Mustang was backed into the garage behind the victim, and disconcertingly, it was running. The Detective couldn't yet see the exhaust heaving from the tailpipe, but he could smell it. On the one hand, that was a good sign: No one had touched the crime scene—if it was a crime scene. On the other hand, the last thing the investigators needed was to inhale carbon monoxide, the one element of exhaust no one could smell.

On his way over, the Detective had called in an evidence

technician he'd worked with before, a young black man who'd moved from Atlanta and settled in the spreading suburbs with his wife and twin daughters. The technician waved to the Detective and called, "The car's locked, but I got another set of keys from the husband."

"Locked, is it?"

The Detective nodded to the uniformed officer. She was thirtyish, with orange-red hair tucked under her cap. She nodded back and briefed him: A Mr. Robert Malcolm Clark had arrived home from work, opened the garage door, and seen his wife lying on the floor; he ran to his neighbor, who placed the 911 call; the husband was in the house waiting for the Detective; the neighbor said she'd be happy to answer questions. The Detective thanked the officer, then stepped under the tape and into the garage, where he could see the victim, sprawled on the floor, her arms in the lazy semaphore of sleep. She lay right by the car, near the driver's side door, as if she'd just climbed out, closed the door behind her, and made herself comfortable on the concrete floor—though that would have been an odd thing to do: close the door and leave the car running.

"Not much room to negotiate here, is there?" the Detective said to the evidence tech.

"Sure isn't," the tech said. "That's why I'm going to the passenger door to open the car. Besides, I might smear some important prints while I'm at it."

The tech gingerly stepped over the victim and around the Mustang. He must have barely beat the Detective there because he was just sliding on his latex gloves. The Detective peered in through the window, spotting what appeared to be a full set of keys hanging from a rabbit's foot keychain. Long time ago, he had a girlfriend who carried one of those. The tech, meanwhile, slid the extra car key into the passenger-door lock and pulled the door open without touching the handle, though he did have to grasp the door's edge.

"Before you shut the ignition," the Detective called, "do me a favor and check the gauges."

The evidence tech leaned way into the Mustang, then pulled back out. "The car's in PARK," he said, "and the engine heat indicator is so far past H, I'm surprised the thing hasn't burned up."

"The gas level?"

"A quarter tank," the tech said, adding, "Maybe I should get a weekend job with Avis?"

"Right," the Detective said, and scribbled down "1/4 tank," curious just how much gas the car had burned.

"Can I turn off the engine now?" the tech asked, and when the Detective said yes, the tech reached across and turned the key to OFF, taking care to hold it by the edges. He left the keys dangling against the rabbit's foot, a piece of evidence he would later bag and label in his systematic collection.

"That's better," the tech said. "You'll want to take a look inside the car at some point, Detective. Not only were the doors locked, the windows were, too. Just be careful. I plan to take prints from every surface of that car."

"Wonder how tight the seal was?" the Detective said. "Bet the air inside was safer than the air outside."

"Did anyone tell you there are two victims?" the evidence tech asked.

"No. All I heard was 'possible suicide.' Husband found his wife in the garage."

"So no one told you the dog died, too?"

"The dog?" the Detective said.

"Sure thing," the evidence tech said. "Right over here by its bowl."

The Detective circled the rear of the Mustang, surveying the garage as he did so. He noted the tools scattered across the top of a dusty workbench and a door that appeared to lead into the house. An ordinary garage, he thought, maybe cleaner than most. And then he saw the dog, a rusty black

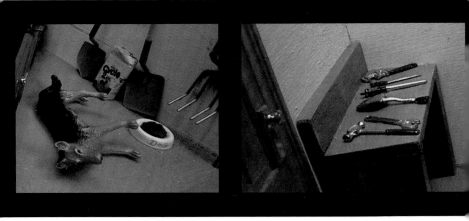

shepherd lying right by his kibble. A small "huh" escaped the Detective.

Like the victim, the dog lay as if sleeping. "Beautiful dog," the Detective said. "Kind of sad to see it this way." Why was it easier to mourn animals than people? The Detective pulled a pair of latex gloves from his inside pocket and slid them onto his hands. Later, he'd have to discuss with the evidence tech whether they should take the dog as evidence. For now, he handled it with care, scarcely touching it as he looked for any obvious signs of trauma, signs that the victim had run over him as she backed into the garage, but he saw none.

He asked the tech, "No other surprises, right?"

"The responding officer said just these two."

"All right. So you're starting on the photos?"

"I am. Anything special you want me to take?"

"May as well get the dog. I doubt the ME will. Otherwise, just do your usual thorough job."

The evidence tech began photographing the scene, recording every detail both inside and outside the garage. The

Detective removed his gloves—rolling the used pair into a bundle and labeling them with his Sharpie, just in case the lab later needed to check them for trace evidence—and made his way back to the victim. He squatted in the space between her head and her outstretched arm, so he could get a better look. She was middle-aged and what his wife would call "well-kept," her hair recently cut, her fingernails manicured, and she wore what the Detective could now see was a night-gown—a fancy summer nightgown, for that matter, with its lacy straps and cotton-candy colors. She appeared to be lying in some kind of mess—feces, it looked like, dog shit. And there was a cut over her right eye.

He pressed up from the floor and scanned the room. Could be she didn't cut herself in the garage at all. Could be he would find evidence she cut herself in the house and came out to the garage to drive herself to the doctor. Still, he searched for something head-height, something her head-height: a shelf, a garage-door track, anything hanging from the ceiling or protruding from the walls. He noted nothing she might have walked into, but he did see many things that could have been used to strike her: the gardening tools hanging on the walls and the wrenches and hammer lying on the worktable. The Detective said, "Take all of the tools as evidence."

The Detective stooped to look again at her face. Her eyes were half-closed, as the eyes of the dead never close fully, and he could see a bright red discoloration where her face pressed against the cool concrete floor. The Detective tried not to hypothesize too soon, but this sure looked like carbon monoxide poisoning to him, and that more often than not meant suicide. But gassers, as he thought of them, seldom stepped outside the car to die. They sat inside, where the seats were soft and they could listen to the radio or the CD player, where they could switch off the ignition if they had a

change of heart or mind. Unless, of course, you were afraid you would change your mind. Then you might lock yourself in the garage but out of the car. Or, he supposed, someone else might lock you in the garage but out of the car. He reminded himself to check all the doors—car doors, garage door, kitchen door—to see how each opened and closed, how each locked—to see if the victim could have walked out of the garage if she had chosen.

There was no doubt. This was a medical examiner's case, so the Detective called the ME's office. Shadytown was large enough, and there were enough sudden, unexplained, unnatural, or criminal deaths, that the city employed one medical examiner pathologist, assisted by several medical examiner investigators. The pathologist, a trained physician, conducted autopsies and made final determinations about the time, cause, and manner of death. The medical examiner investigators, highly trained but not physicians, oversaw crime scenes and made preliminary determinations. The Detective recognized the voice of the man assigned to this case, an older forensic investigator who, the Detective thought, anyone would have mistaken for a country doctor.

The evidence technician needed to photograph the area where the Detective stood, so the Detective ducked under the tape and out of the garage. He reminded himself that the victim's death could have been accidental. She could have climbed from her car, closed the garage door, returned to the car to shut it off but found it locked, and in her hurry, slipped in the feces. But why would the victim close the garage door before she turned off the car? Who did that?

The Detective took a step away from the garage and studied the door. He saw no garage-door pull hanging down, but he also saw no remote-control button on either side. Security-conscious people didn't have a convenience switch outside their garages, he'd noted. So he ducked his head inside, checking first one side of the garage door and then the other. There, in the hard-to-reach corner by the nose of the car, he found the automatic opener, a rectangular white button. The victim could have saved herself if she'd simply pressed it. Must be a remote control in her car, and one in the husband's car, which was, the Detective noticed, still dinging on the driveway. He toed open the door and found the remote clipped to the visor. Having no idea whether this remote would become evidence, he tried not to destroy any latent prints. He pushed the button with his thumbnail rather than pressing it with his thumb, and the door slowly cranked down.

"Hey!" the uniformed officer shouted.

"Sorry," the Detective said and thumbnailed the door back up. He climbed from the car and said, "Don't have one of these things for my garage. Do you?"

"No, but I don't have a garage, either."

"If you did, would you back your car into it?"

"Maybe. Some people prefer backing in to backing out. My sister does."

"Your sister has a garage?"

"Her husband does," the officer said. "She keeps her car in the driveway or on the street."

The Detective scratched his head. "So this victim's husband found her, right?"

"Right." The officer pulled the notebook from her pants pocket and checked it. "Mr. Robert Malcolm Clark came home from work at five, opened the garage…"

"With his remote from the sedan out there in the driveway?"

"I didn't ask," the officer said. "He just said he opened the garage door, saw his wife, and ran to the neighbor's house. Asked her to call 911."

"He didn't move his wife? Didn't try to resuscitate her?"

"Not that he said. He said he found her at 5:00 p.m., and the 911 call came in at 5:02. Wouldn't leave much time for mouth-to-mouth."

"And they both live here, right? They're not separated or anything, are they?"

"No, they live here—with their son." She checked her notes again. "Robert Malcolm, Jr."

"This Mustang their car?"

"Yes, sir. I ran the plates. They're valid. Car's registered to her."

"Not to the son?" the Detective asked. "Not really the car you buy for the wife."

"Maybe not for your wife," the officer said. She let her answer sit, then added, "The son's only 10."

"That is a little young for driving," the Detective said. "So, do you think this is Mr. Clark's garage? Think it was usually his car in there, not hers?"

"Couldn't say."

"Which neighbor called 911?"

"The one right here, with the driveway and garage just like the Clarks'." The officer looked again at her notebook.

"Name's Nancy Scott."

"You interview her?"

"I did. She said she saw Mrs. Clark around nine this morning. Far as we know, she was the last one to see Mrs. Clark alive."

"What was she doing?"

"Mrs. Scott was watering her yard."

The Detective looked at the officer levelly.

"You mean Mrs. Clark?" the officer asked. "She was backing her car into the garage. She told Mrs. Scott she wasn't feeling well and wasn't going in to work."

"Did Nancy Scott say what the victim was wearing?"

"Her nightgown. A white nightgown with pink stripes and a pink bow in front with long, pink streamers."

"Just what she's wearing now," he said. "And all of this seemed normal to Mrs. Scott?"

"You mean Mrs. Clark not feeling well?"

"I mean Mrs. Clark backing her car into the garage. Did she always move her car into the garage when her husband was out and she was home?"

"I didn't ask," the officer said. "I did tell her you'd want to speak with her, and I asked her not to talk to anyone."

"Thanks. I will want to talk with her." The evidence tech had finished his photos and was taking measurements of the scene and scratching them in his sketchbook. "I'm curious," the Detective said. "Do you think the victim just closed the garage door and locked herself out of her car by accident?"

"I don't know," the officer replied.

"Neither do I."

"Clear case of carbon monoxide poisoning," the ME said. "You can see what it did." He gestured toward the pressure points—the areas that had borne the victim's weight during the hours she had lain prone on the concrete floor. They were white, but around them, where her blood had slowly pooled since her heart stopped pumping, her skin had turned a distinctive red. "Oxygen bound to hemoglobin turns it red. Carbon dioxide turns it purple. But when carbon monoxide binds to hemoglobin, the blood turns bright cherry red. Where the blood settled, you can see that bright color. The lividity and rigor mortis suggest she died maybe eight hours ago, about 9:00 a.m."

"Anyone move her?"

"Now that's an interesting question," the ME said. "The answer is no, but she might have moved herself, or tried to. I've got to bag her hands." The MEs always used paper bags for the purpose, so any biological evidence on the victim's hands would dry slowly in the air. If he bagged her hands in plastic, bacteria would grow in the humid mini-ecosphere, ruining whatever trace evidence remained. "You see the way her arms are lying? Sort of like a baby sleeping? But also like a baby crawling?"

"She was trying to crawl out of the garage?" the Detective asked. "Toward that door over there?"

"Or she was flailing," the ME said. "I don't see any obvious contusions or abrasions, but the pathologist will get a better look in the morgue."

"So, she flailed on the garage floor until she passed out." As the Detective said this, he couldn't help but imagine someone pushing her back down, a boot to her back.

"We won't know for sure until the autopsy," the ME said, "but I believe she's lying in dog doo."

The Detective sighed. "You know the dog died, too?"

"That's a shame," the ME said, and let a moment's sorrow pass before adding, "Here's another thing. See that cut over her left eye?"

"I saw it," the Detective said.

"It might have sent her to the emergency room for stitches, but it didn't kill her," the ME said. "Not much blood, either. Just this drop here. Want my theory?"

The Detective nodded.

"She slipped on the feces, hit her head, and lost consciousness—maybe recovered just enough to try to scramble off the floor."

The Detective stepped carefully across the victim, knelt, and lowered his head to get a look at the victim's feet.

"She's wearing shoes," he said. Simple, low-heeled shoes, the sort women sometimes keep at the office for comfort or in their cars for driving. "Shoes, not slippers. If that's dog feces she's lying in, I guess this is feces on her sole as well."

The Detective fished his oldest pencil from his pocket and pressed the tip into the excreta caked behind the heel of her shoe. It was black as mud where it had oxidized, ochre under the surface. Released, the sharp smell cut through the half-combusted carbon that still filled the air. "That's ripe," the Detective said. He wrapped his pencil in his handkerchief and slipped it, reluctantly, back into his pocket. "Must have been a sick puppy."

"Looks that way."

"Be sure to take samples of the feces," the Detective called out to the tech. "And you may as well take some of the dog food, too. Just in case."

The Detective scanned the corner of the garage where the victim lay. She was close enough to the workbench, her head could have struck that as she fell. But the ME said, "If you're looking for what she hit, it's this toolbox over here."

The Detective followed the ME's gaze and saw a wooden toolbox nestled on the floor near the garage door, blood on the far corner, the uppermost corner. To the tech, he said, "Be sure to run a field-presumptive blood test on this toolbox here." He turned back to the ME. "No other trauma?"

"None that I can see. The pathologist will tell you more once the victim's in the morgue," the ME said. "Her name's Helen Clark, by the way. I'm going to go ahead and transport her."

The Detective nodded and stood up. He stepped under the tape and out of the garage, glad for the fresh air. He couldn't help but shake his head. He sometimes thought every death contained its own private joke. But locked out of a running car, and from the looks of it, your own running car?

The Detective lifted the CRIME SCENE tape so the transport team could pass under. The evidence tech chalked an outline around the victim, then stepped back so the transport team could remove the body. The ME was busy writing in his notebook, but the Detective interrupted, "So how long does it take, carbon monoxide poisoning?"

"In a garage with the door closed?" the ME asked. "With the car running, the air is saturated in five to ten minutes. It's minutes, not hours, if that's the bone you're worrying."

"That's one of them," the Detective said, adding, "You think the dog was poisoned? My dog doesn't make indoors if it can help it."

"Like we said, the dog could have been sick. I don't think you'll learn much by examining it," the ME said.

"We could send it to the State U.," the Detective said. "They've got a Department of Animal Science."

"Think they'd autopsy it?" the ME asked.

"Sure do." The Detective nodded, then turned to the evidence tech, who was sketching the entire crime scene. "You'll want to get your camera out again and get a shot of this mess here." The Detective indicated the splash of feces.

"I noticed a few things that might interest you," the tech said. "I tried the door to the house." He pinched his fingers in a delicate O, showing that he'd gripped the stem, not the knob, to protect latent prints. "And it's locked. I've still got the husband's keys, so I found one that fit, but I didn't unlock the door yet. I thought you'd want to."

"Let me see," the Detective said. The tech handed him the correct key, and using it, the Detective opened the door easily; no one had thrown the deadbolt.

"So she could have walked right into her house if she'd had her keys," the Detective said. "But why use keys? If she walked out simply to bring in the car, why lock the door? Did she always lock the kitchen door after her?"

"There's a sliding bolt lock on the garage door, too," the tech said. "I noticed the eye while taking photos." He pointed toward the simple hole in the doorframe that the bolt slid into, then gazed overhead. "The bolt's up there, on the door."

"Even if the bolt was locked," the Detective said, "she could have slid the bolt, pushed the button, and walked out." Unless the switch didn't work. "You're going to take latents from that garage-door switch, right? Let me know when you do, because I need to see if it works."

He pulled on a clean pair of latex gloves and used the husband's keys to open the driver's door without touching the handle. Then he slid into Mrs. Clark's seat and gave the interior a cursory inspection. The Mustang had an automatic lock, as well as buttons that slid in and out. The windows also locked, and as the tech had told him, the window lock was on, which surprised the Detective. His children were grown, but even when they were young, he never used the window lock. He checked in the foot wells and under the seats for the victim's purse, which he did not find. If the victim had driven the car last, he decided, she hadn't planned to drive far. He didn't find any stashed bottles either, and when he shook the commute-a-cup, he heard no sloshing. Inside the armrest, he found $1.77 in loose change and three cassette tapes: *Dusty in Memphis*, *The Very Best of Aretha Franklin*, and *The Art of Cecilia Bartoli*. The officer was right: This was the victim's car. The Detective then flipped the visors down, finding only the vanity mirror on the passenger's side, the garage door remote on the driver's.

The Detective climbed out, reflexively stepping over the space the victim had occupied. It was growing dark, so he told the tech to make a note that he had turned the light on at 6:07 p.m. Then he pulled the string of the hanging bulb. "So we'll want prints from the kitchen door, the bolt lock, and the switch; areas around the ignition; and the remote device on the visor." The Detective would make sure they took elim-ination fingerprints—prints from the victim, her husband, and her son. Once he had eliminated the prints of those who had innocent access to the crime scene, he could search for the prints of someone who might not be so innocent. "When you've got those, lower the door and dust it panel by panel. See if the victim pounded on the door." He started to leave, but turned back. "After you've checked for prints, go through the car again. Make sure there's no note."

The Detective found Mr. Clark talking on the phone, call-ing members of his family, he said when he hung up. When the Detective asked him to describe his wife's health the past few days, Mr. Clark said she had been well until that morn-ing, when she complained of an upset stomach. The Detective asked what medications she took, and Mr. Clark said, "Nothing but Advil." When asked for Mrs. Clark's psy-chiatrist's number, Mr. Clark said she didn't have one, though he could provide that of their primary care physician. "Mind if I look in her medicine chest?" the Detective asked, though when he did, he found nothing but Neosporin, cosmetics, and a few bottles of outdated Cipro and Percocet. "For surgery on her torn rotator cuff," Mr. Clark said.

No matter how benignly the Detective asked his questions, Mr. Clark would not say his wife drank or was depressed. Several times he said his parents were picking his son up at camp, but how would he ever tell him?

"Enemies?" the Detective asked, and Mr. Clark said, "None." Before departing, the Detective apologized for asking if Mr. Clark had found a note.

"Note?" Mr. Clark asked. "What do you mean 'note'?"

"So she left no note?"

"My wife wasn't expecting to die," Mr. Clark answered. "She didn't leave a note."

Mrs. Scott told the Detective the same story she'd told the

uniformed officer: Around nine in the morning, she saw her neighbor backing her car into the garage, asked her how she was (not well), and saw the garage door close. Mrs. Scott claimed she didn't know her neighbor well enough to say whether she usually left her house by the front door or by the garage, and had no idea if she was in the habit of locking every door behind her. The only thing she could say for certain is that Mrs. Clark kept her car in the driveway, not the garage.

By the time he got back to the garage, the evidence tech had bagged and tagged the evidence and was beginning to take latent prints, brushing graphite dust onto the kitchen door. The tech said, "I already dusted that switch."

"Right. The switch," the Detective said, and pressed the button. The door began its robotic descent. "Well, that doesn't explain it either."

"The toolbox was positive for blood on the benzidine color test," the tech said.

"No surprise there."

"What do you want me to do with the dog? Leave it for Mr. Clark to take care of?"

"Make a little room in the refrigerator?" the Detective said wryly. "What we're going to do, we'll take it to Shadytown's Department of Animal Science. I know a guy there who'll autopsy it. If we find poison in the victim, we might find poison in the dog. Maybe she wanted the dog to die with her, or maybe they both ate the same poisoned food. You just never know."

The next morning, the Detective attended the autopsy, to answer any questions the pathologist might have. The process began with the victim in the state in which she had been found, on her stomach and clothed in her nightgown. When the pathologist turned the body over, she exposed the feces smeared all over the victim's gown and her swollen, bright red face. That lividity was fixed, the pathologist said, meaning now that the blood had settled, it wasn't going anywhere, and the pressure points were consistent with the position in which the victim had been found: It seemed she had not been moved. Other than the cut above the right eye, the pathologist found no trauma whatsoever and no sign of struggle, and no blood or skin under the victim's fingernails. The pathologist did note slight abrasions on the victim's arms, as if she had flailed on the floor. She found no evidence Helen Clark had been sexually assaulted. The pathologist put the time of death around 9:30 a.m. and hypothesized the blow to the victim's head had knocked her unconscious.

"Should find bleeding in the cranial cavity," the pathologist said, but when she opened the skull, she discovered no sign of concussion. "The victim may have been dazed, but nothing more."

Dissatisfied, the Detective asked how someone not intending suicide could slip and not get up, simply because she was dazed. The pathologist said, "Carbon monoxide poisoning's sneaky. I hear about entire families discovered in their weekend homes, all of them gone only minutes after they started up a faulty heater."

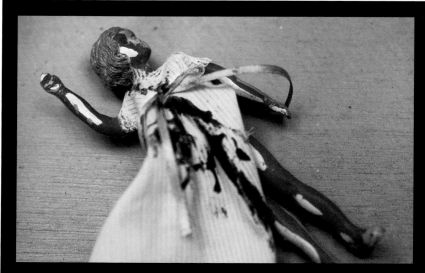

As for ABO typing, the victim's blood would be typed later in the day, as would the two blood samples taken from the scene—the blood on the floor and that on the toolbox. "But you're expecting no surprises there, are you?" the pathologist asked. For toxicology, the Detective would have to wait at least a week, though the pathologist put her money on carbon monoxide poisoning. That is exactly what the toxicology report indicated. No other poisons were found in the victim's system, which is also what the Department of Animal Science reported: no toxins other than carbon monoxide.

The only prints found inside or outside the garage belonged to the Clarks. Only Mrs. Clark's prints were found around the ignition of her car, and only her prints were found on the garage-door bolt lock. Everyone's prints were found on the doorknobs into and out of the kitchen—Mrs. Clark, Mr. Clark, and Robert Malcolm Clark, Jr. There were very few prints on the garage door panels, certainly no indication Mrs. Clark had pounded the door.

The following day, the Detective canvassed the neighbors, but they offered little new information. They saw no one else on the property that day and believed Mrs. Clark to be a lovely neighbor who played a great game of tennis. Mrs. Clark's boss at the department store confirmed that she had called in sick around 8:00 a.m. that morning, but no, she seemed to have no enemies, no problems she discussed. The woman did take her sick days, the boss said, but when she was there, she was a hard worker. For what little it was worth, the boss added, pink was her favorite color, peony pink. During a second interview, Mrs. Scott did mention "that little problem Helen Clark had a few years ago," and when the Detective searched the records, he found a three-year-old DUI arrest. But tests revealed no alcohol in her blood when she died. The Detective did ask Mr. Clark about the arrest, and he said, "That was one time, three years ago, for Christ's sake. My wife was no drinker."

A dozen different ways the Detective imagined Helen Clark's end. In one she pulled the Mustang into the garage, shut off the engine, and went into the house. It was sometime later, perhaps after she discovered she had no milk for her coffee, that she got back in the car and started it up again, but oops, she forgot her purse, hurried out and slipped, the car door closing behind her. In another, she was worried about the dog and rushed from the car before turning it off. In some versions, she deliberately left the car running, deliberately locked herself out, slipping only when she'd had a change of heart.

In the end, he settled for what could be determined. Mrs. Clark backed her Mustang into her garage around 9:00 a.m. the morning of May 9. She closed the garage door and got out of the car, leaving the doors and windows locked and the engine running, whether on purpose or by accident remained unanswered. She apparently slipped on dog feces, cutting her head on the toolbox as she fell. She did not lose consciousness, but was dazed. She tried to get up, but succumbed to carbon monoxide poisoning within minutes, as did the dog. He was tagged "Jerry Lee Lewis."

3. The Store

The *Country Store:* That's what the glowing sign overhead and the blue neon script in the display window announced. As far as the Detective was concerned, the name underscored that this, the oldest and most urban of Shadytown's suburbs, was far from the country. The store sat at the far end of a corner mall—two strip malls that merged at a fast-food restaurant strategically sited at a busy intersection. Driving south from the restaurant, as the Detective and his partner did, you passed a nail salon, a dry cleaner, and a pet store, all of them dark and gated at 10:22 p.m. And then you came to The Country Store, a mom-and-pop convenience store that had managed to survive despite competition from the chain stores. Over the years, the Detective and his partner had stopped by for coffee or Crazy Glue or Tums. The Detective knew Mabel, the mom of mom-and-pop, better than he knew Hal, but he liked them both. The call had said two shooting victims—likely a double homicide—and the Detective prayed he wouldn't find either of them when he walked in.

Four emergency medical technicians were leaving The Country Store as the Detective's partner pulled up. One carried a rolled-up stretcher against his shoulder, like a flag or standard, and seeing that the EMTs were taking no one to the hospital, the Detective's partner said, "That's that."

"Sure is," the Detective said. "Looks like we can scratch the *likely.*"

It was a medical examiner's case now, so the Detective pulled out his cell phone and called the ME's office, after that calling in the evidence technicians. The Detective and his

partner then climbed from the car and made their way through the motley crowd of people attracted to the red lights of the squad car and the two ambulances. The bystanders seemed to have come from the apartment block that marked the end of the strip mall, and from the restaurant at the corner. Some even came by car, pulling into the driveway and cruising slowly past the scene.

One of the uniformed officers who'd responded to the 911 call was spinning out yellow CRIME SCENE tape, trying to establish a perimeter around the front of the store. The other officer stood before the glass door the EMTs had just exited, telling people, "Please step behind the yellow tape. We need to secure the crime scene."

That officer told the Detective and his partner, "The EMTs just confirmed they're both dead."

"The EMTs move the bodies?" the Detective asked.

"No," the officer said. "I watched them carefully. The only thing they did was touch the carotid and leave."

"So who do we have in there?"

"One's the clerk. The other's an obvious robber—with a mask and a shotgun on a sling. Register and safe are open; there's cash all over the floor."

"The clerk—it isn't Mabel or Hal, is it?"

"They're the owners?"

The Detective nodded, as did his partner, and the officer said, "I don't know. Young guy, whoever it is, twentysomething, I'd say."

"Well then it's not Mabel or Hal," the Detective said. "But it could be one of the family. They employ a lot of relatives."

"Hope it's not the son," his partner said.

"You check the store?" the Detective asked. "You searched the back rooms, the bathroom?"

"Everything's secure. Back door's locked with a burglar bar."

"What about our caller?" the Detective asked.

"He's right over there." The officer indicated the end of the parking lot, and the Detective saw a skinny guy in an undershirt, shorts, and heavy sandals leaning against the hood of a Honda Civic. His arms were wrapped across his chest, as if it were cold, but it certainly wasn't cold tonight. It was almost August, and the heat hadn't broken in weeks, not even at night. Everyone was trying to get cool. Somewhere in the city, a fire hydrant was open, and parents and kids were running through the spray. Somewhere in the city, kids were climbing chain-link fences, sneaking into public pools after-hours.

"Want me to take his statement?" his partner asked.

"Yeah, sure," the Detective said. His partner was a good guy, even if aggravating at times. Maybe the Detective had had to teach him not to swear, but he seldom had to tell him how to do the job—unlike the uniformed officer, who was still trying to establish a perimeter.

The Detective strode into the crowd gathered on the concrete walk. They seemed both fascinated and afraid, pressing up against the glass, then backing away. One man even had a small boy astride his shoulders, and the Detective took the time to say, "You don't want the boy to see this. I promise you." Then the Detective raised his voice, saying, "Please back off and let the officer secure the scene. Please, back off."

The Detective helped the officer loop the tape around a stanchion and attach the end to the accordion gates Hal and Mabel hardly used. It was the rare day they weren't open 24 hours. To the officer, he said, "Once you secure the storefront, I'd like the parking lot secured, too. Got to get these prying eyes out of here. Besides, who knows if there's evidence out here?" The Detective didn't love the role of boss, but as senior detective, he couldn't avoid it. Once on the scene, he had the job of directing the uniformed officers and calling in staff. "And one more thing. When you're done here, rope off the delivery entrance, too."

The officer nodded, and the Detective rolled on a pair of latex gloves and entered the store, where, thank God, it was cool. Hal maintained a few well-stocked aisles at the front, keeping the register and clerk's counter at the back, a nice, big pastry case dividing the aisles from the checkout and self-serve coffee area. The Detective walked back, past the front aisles, to the first body, the robber, or would-be robber, for cash lay all around him—tens, twenties, fives, singles—all the small denominations a convenience store takes in, the infrequent fifty or hundred earning careful scrutiny. The robber lay on his back by the pastry case, his sawed-off shotgun in plain sight, his face covered with a stocking-cap mask. The second body—a clerk the Detective didn't recognize (it wasn't Hal and Mabel's son, that much he knew)—slumped on the floor, the trail of blood on the tiles behind him indicating he'd slid down the wall after he was shot.

The Detective grimaced and circled around the robber. One spent shotgun shell lay right at the man's feet. The Detective squatted down to take a closer look. Because the shell could have prints on it, he poked a pencil inside the case and lifted it slightly. He took it to be a shell for a wide-bore gun. He lowered it gently to the floor and moved closer to the counter to study the robber. The shotgun he took to be a 12-gauge, the widest bore made. It could shoot some mean shot. The robber had hitched it to a coat-hanger sling, which he had looped over his right shoulder. The gun would have hung under his trench coat, so all he had to do was open his coat and swing the gun up to make demands of the clerk. Could be the clerk saw the guy enter and knew he was trouble from the get-go, even if he hadn't put on his mask yet. A trench coat. On a night like this? Could be the clerk had time to screw up his courage as the man strode to the back of the store. If so, it was too bad. Cowardice might have saved the clerk and saved his family heartbreak.

The left side of the coat was soaked with blood, and the floor was wet with it. The right side was bloody, too, suggesting there might be another wound. Though he couldn't see the guy's face, what with the stocking cap pulled over it, the Detective could see just enough of the guy's hands and neck to guess he wasn't your usual brash, twentysomething robber. The stocking cap and the coat-hanger sling fingered this guy as a lifer—a professional—though *pro* suggested more skill and polish than the Detective credited this guy with.

The Detective took a last look—the cheap checked shirt, the funny eyes on the cap (what were they about?), the paper sack at the guy's head, bills scattered over the floor. The Detective stretched himself up and peered over the counter at the clerk. It wasn't hard to see the weapon the clerk had used: a handgun lay near his feet. The register was open and the coffeepot was hot, as a light touch with the back of his hand proved. The clock above the clerk's head read 10:07. Reflexively, the Detective checked his own watch, noting it was now 10:56 p.m. The clock's face was smashed in the middle, as was the victim's. The Detective could make out three wounds to the man's face—mean wounds, one right through the forehead. Well, the robber hadn't shot slugs, the Detective figured, more likely buckshot, a spray of lead balls, one of them bound to hit home.

He heard the door open behind him and turned quickly, another reflex, only to see his partner walking toward him. The partner said, "Shootout, huh? Attempted robbery more than likely."

The Detective had to smile at his instinctive partner, always jumping to conclusions. But of course everything about the scene did say *attempted robbery*. Everything said *shootout*. "We're going to have to get a closer look at the weapons and ammunition, buddy, but yeah, I'd say that's what this looks like. Never knew Harold Owens kept a gun in the store."

"You blame him?"

"Maybe. Let's hope the gun was registered and secured." The Detective looked again at the victim and his vicious wounds. "The clerk must have felt pretty sure of his shot or pretty angry at being held up to risk *that*."

"What do you think? Double ought buckshot from a 12-gauge shotgun?"

"You're saying this guy was a cop?" the Detective asked.

"You know me better than that," his partner said. "I'm saying our guy used the same ammunition cops use."

"I won't argue that. Like I said, we'll need to get a closer look when the evidence techs get here," the Detective said. "What'd you learn from our caller?"

"Not much," the partner said. "He's the only car in the parking lot when he pulls in about 10:10. He goes into the store to buy a six-pack of soda plus some ice cream for the wife and finds the two bodies. He bolts from the store, finds his cell phone in the car, and calls 911. Then he climbs in his car, locks the doors and windows, and waits. He saw no one in or around the store before or when he walked in, though he did tell a few people to stay away before our uniformed officers arrived. He seems a little worried we'll want to pin this on him."

"You straighten him out?"

"I did, but I also got his card, with his work and cell phone printed on it and his home phone written in ink. He works for the transportation authority, dispatching trains and processing delays."

His partner held the card between two short fingers. He was short, and everything about him was short—his legs, his arms, his nose, his hair, and of course, his fingers. The Detective didn't always notice it, but when he did, he was always surprised.

"And you sent him home?"

"Not before I asked you."

The Detective smiled to himself and gazed at the floor. "What do you know? I've taught you something."

Avoiding the doorknob, the Detective coaxed open the door to the storage room and back office. The desk lamp was lit, so the Detective didn't need his flashlight to find the emergency telephone list. Hal's number was at the top. The Detective flipped open his phone and dialed, only to get endless ringing. Well, maybe the man was on vacation. The walk-in freezer rumbled as it started up, and the Detective rejoined his partner, who was gazing up at the security camera.

"You're not posing for that thing?" the Detective asked.

"What if I was?" his partner said. "Actually, I was just thinking that if we're lucky, we'll have the whole thing on tape."

"If we're lucky," the Detective said. "We talked to Hal about getting a security system, didn't we?"

"That's what I remember, but I don't think he ever did. Everybody's cutting corners these days."

The Detective nodded. He didn't know about everybody, but he was cutting corners. He hit redial, and this time someone answered. The Detective explained who he was, and

Mabel (he was almost certain it was Mabel) told him to wait. Hal picked up, and the Detective identified himself. "There was an attempted robbery at your store. And there's been a shooting."

"I know, I know. One of my neighbors told me. He drove by and saw the police cars, the ambulances. I've just been on the phone with my sister. It's her son who was working tonight. She's coming over and then we're coming over. But you've got to tell me…"

"He died, Hal. I'm sorry," the Detective said. "He didn't stand much of a chance against a shotgun blast."

"How many times did I tell him? Don't resist, don't resist."

The Detective didn't ask the man why he kept a gun around if he didn't want his clerks resisting. He said, "We don't really know yet how this thing played out. You know what I mean, Hal? Could be resisting had nothing to do with it."

"My sister," Hal said. "What am I going to say to my sister?"

The Detective couldn't imagine what Hal would say. He asked a practical question instead: "What's your nephew's name?"

"Charles," Harold Owens said. "Charles Greene. He works days as a job estimator in construction. He asked me if he could work nights because he was saving to get married."

"I'm really sorry, Hal," the Detective said. "Really sorry. We'll be here when you get here. We'll talk then."

The Detective gazed toward the street, relieved to see the parking lot empty of bystanders, but not completely empty. The two officers stood out front, and the ME was striding up to the door. She carried a messenger satchel and was wearing scrubs, perhaps because they were loose and therefore cool; the Detective didn't know. He did know she wasn't long for the department: She'd gotten into medical school. His partner opened the door for her, and she greeted them, "Detectives," and set to work. She confirmed both men were dead and dead only a short time, given the warmth of their bodies and the minor degree of blood coagulation.

"I'd say the clerk died when the clock died, at 10:07 p.m. The suspect died a few minutes later. Were the EMTs here?"

"Sure were," the Detective said.

"Well, that's why," she said. "The uniformed officer thought the suspect might still be alive."

She wanted to look at the wounds—the detective could see her eagerness—but she had to photograph the bodies first, to record their locations, positions, and conditions. She pulled her camera from her messenger satchel and began photographing, starting with long shots of each body, trying to capture the surroundings, anything that would give the viewer a sense of proportion. Slowly she got closer to each body, closer to the wounds.

"These are awful," she said, as she shot the clerk's face. She was shooting close enough that her photos would show the entry wounds as craters. When she finished shooting, she returned to the suspect and lifted his coat and shirt just enough to reveal the entry wound, ringed in black, singed and abraded as the bullet pierced the skin.

"Just missed his heart is my guess," the ME said. "But it may have hit his pulmonary aorta. There's a lot of blood on the coat, but I bet most of his bleeding was internal. And he's got a second wound. That's why there's blood on the right side." She lifted the body just enough to check. "Yeah, around his kidneys."

"Mind checking for ID?" the Detective asked.

"Not at all."

She searched the pockets of the trench coat first, which were empty, as were the front pockets of his trousers. She reached under the body and checked the back pockets as well. Not a bit squeamish, the Detective noticed.

"Nothing?" the Detective asked.

"Not even a ticket stub," she said.

"No car keys?" the Detective's partner asked.

"Somehow I don't think he was planning to walk home," the Detective said.

"He had an accomplice," the partner said. "Someone was sitting out there waiting for him. Drove away when the shooting started. That's what I think."

The evidence technicians had arrived while the ME was performing her preliminary examination of the two bodies. Their mobile crime laboratory was parked on the street, and they stood just inside the front door, waiting for the ME to finish. She pulled her clipboard out of her messenger bag and began jotting down information about each decedent. She wrote "John Doe" for the suspect and asked the Detective if he had a name for the clerk.

"Greene," he said. "Charles Greene, or so we think. We'll get a positive ID from the owner when he gets here."

"And we know who discovered the body?" she asked.

The partner flipped out the business card so she could take down the information. To the evidence techs she called, "Hiya, I'm about finished," and one of them came over and chalked the positions of the bodies.

"We've got to photograph the scene," the other one said.

The Detective nodded and said, "Come on, buddy," and he and his partner stepped outside the store, the ME joining them.

"Isn't there supposed to be a light on those cameras?" the partner asked. "A little green light that tells you the camera's playing?"

"I don't know," the Detective said. "Wouldn't that give the show away? Mr. Criminal, you're being recorded now."

"I'm just saying there's no little green light on that surveillance camera."

"So maybe all the camera did," the ME said, "was give the suspect a reason to pull a mask over his face."

The Detective suggested that Mabel and Hal's sister, Sonia, wait outside the store, while he took Hal in and asked him to ID the clerk's body. The evidence techs had finished their photos by then and were measuring and sketching the store. They stopped their work for a moment to let Hal pass. His store had been robbed before—four times in the past year—and the thieves had been armed before, but no one had ever been shot in his store. He swayed on his feet when he reached the pastry case at the back of the store, and the Detective had to steady him.

"Yeah, that's Charles," Harold Owens said. "Oh, my God, that's my nephew, Charles."

The Detective waited a decent moment, then said, "We need to walk through and make sure nothing else has been stolen, you understand?"

Hal said he did, so they walked through the back of the store, and then the front, Hal saying, "No, no, no, nothing's missing." Then they peered into the space behind the counter where the safe gaped open and empty.

Hal said, "You know, I only gave the combination to a few people—Mabel and a few others. Otherwise, I come in midshift and end of shift and empty the drawer into the safe or make a drop at the bank. I gave the combination to Charles just a few weeks ago."

"Is that where you kept the pistol?"

"Sure is," Hal said.

Harold Owens looked again at his nephew, and then at the halo of splattered blood that told him where his nephew had last stood. "Why the hell did I give him that combination? Why? So Mabel and I could have a night to ourselves, not have to come to the store? What kind of reason was that?"

"Hey, hey," the Detective said, and gently guided Hal out of the store, leaving the evidence technicians to continue their work.

Sonia was still weeping in Mabel's arms, the ME standing nearby, plainly uncertain what to do. So the Detective and his partner walked a few feet away.

The partner asked, "Is that surveillance camera working?"

"No," Hal said, "it's not."

The Detective could see Hal tallying his failings, the small compromises he'd made that, in his mind, his family was now paying for.

"It broke down barely a year after we had it installed," Hal said. "Right after the warranty expired. I figured just having it would make them think twice, try some other store instead of mine."

The partner shot the Detective a look, and the Detective nodded, saying only, "Well, it's too bad we don't have a video." He then asked, "Your clock was working, yes?"

Harold Owens said it was, and the Detective asked a more difficult question. "Tell me about the handgun, Hal."

"I bought it seven years ago, when the store was being robbed all the time—at least that's the way it seemed to me.

Before the restaurant moved in on the corner and the stores across the street got fancy on us. Now we're held up, but not so often."

"You're the owner?" the Detective asked. "The gun's registered to you?"

"Yeah, it's mine and it's legal," Harold Owens said. "It's a 9-millimeter Luger. Bought it from Brody's Hunting Gear. You know them?"

"We do," the Detective said, and he and his partner both nodded.

"We'll have to check the registration, and we'll have to hold the gun indefinitely, until we decide we won't need it as evidence. You understand?"

Hal said he did. The Detective added, "We're going to be here maybe another four, five hours. I expect you'll want to be closed for the day. But look, Hal, you're not going to want to clean this store yourself. You might try these guys," and he handed Hal a business card for a crime scene cleanup company. It was lousy Hal had to face this, too.

The Detective led Hal back to his wife and sister. He told them all how sorry he and his partner were and then excused himself. Because the van from the contracted funeral home had arrived, the Detective and his partner walked back into the store, grateful for Hal's air conditioning, and asked the techs if they planned to collect gunshot residue from the bodies' hands. One of the techs said, "I don't think we should run a GSR. It might destroy other evidence. But we could. The hands aren't bagged yet."

"They aren't bagged?" The Detective turned to his partner. "Tell that ME to get in here and deal with these guys' hands. Doesn't she know we're not ready for transport?" He shook his head. "Just because she's off to school, she thinks she can get careless on the job?"

When she returned, the ME recognized her mistake and worked quickly and apologetically. "I'll bag the hands right away."

"And what about gunshot residue?"

"We'll do that at the morgue," she said, and when the Detective seemed dissatisfied, one of the evidence technicians said, "That'd be best. You really don't want to destroy evidence while collecting other evidence."

After the bodies were removed, the evidence technicians continued to work meticulously. With photos and sketches finished, they chose to spiral outwards from the bodies, collecting and securing the weapons first. They confirmed the handgun was a 9-millimeter Luger and the shotgun was 12-gauge and rendered each weapon safe for transport. They sealed the Luger in a handgun transport box, enclosed the sawed-off shotgun in a brown paper evidence bag—a big one. The tech working behind the counter said, "We've got three casings here, each clearly marked '9-m-m'," then put each casing into a cotton-padded pill box.

"Three?" the partner asked. "You think our robber took three shots?"

"We only saw one in the front, didn't we?" The Detective studied the likely trajectory. "And one in the back."

"And one was a flyer," his partner said.

"He hit him low in the back," the Detective said. "At that height, the first thing that would stop a bullet would be the pastry case."

"Would you look at that?" the partner said. "Cracks in the display glass, like a bullet ricocheted around inside."

The Detective peered into the case. "Seek and you shall find."

The closest evidence tech approached, a small gripper in her hands. She opened the case, and following standard procedure, she lifted out the bullet with rubber-padded tongs

without touching the casing, the area most likely to bear prints, placing the bullet in another cotton-padded box.

"That's the pirouette bullet," the Detective's partner said.

"What?" the Detective said.

"That's the reaction-time bullet, the time-to-turn bullet." The partner looked grim. "Charles's first shot hits our robber, but his second doesn't. And that miss gives our robber just enough time to turn, sling his shotgun up, and fire. I know you don't want me to say this, but if Charles had been a better shot, he'd have made it. He wasn't, and he didn't."

"He shouldn't have touched that gun."

"No, he shouldn't have," the partner had to agree.

They circled around the counter and studied the spray of blood.

"What did that shotgun shell say?" the Detective asked the technicians.

"Said '12 gauge' on the base and 'double ought buck' on the plastic," one of the evidence techs answered. "0-0 buck."

"Shoots nine 33-caliber lead balls in a tight spray, making it hard to miss your buck before it runs back into the woods," the Detective said. "Well, you were exactly right, buddy. Not off by a millimeter."

"Hit him at pretty high velocity," the partner said, "judging by the fineness of the spray."

"I'm afraid so. And it looks like six or seven hit him, since only two, maybe three, hit the wall."

The Detective turned away, wearied by the accumulation of random mistakes. He talked with the technicians about the evidence yet to be bagged—the cash, the grocery bag the cash must have been in—and the prints yet to be taken; the weapons and the bag could be printed in the lab, but the register, the counter, and all the door handles would have to be dusted for prints before the technicians left.

He added, "Those 33-caliber balls left in the wall? I'm afraid we'll have to gouge them out."

And then the Detective and his partner left to canvass the neighborhood. The restaurant seemed a good place to start, and then the apartment building.

Early the following morning, the Detective and his partner watched the autopsies. Each body began fully clothed on the slab and was turned over fully clothed. Thus, they saw the robber's first wound, the one that made him turn and shoot, and they saw the large exit wound in Charles Greene's head. They were available to answer any questions, but they also oversaw the collection of gunshot residue, the antimony and barium from the powder that blows back against the shooter's hand. They watched as the pathologist dipped cotton swabs into a dilute nitrous acid solution and brushed one swab against the back of a hand, another against the palm, paying special attention to the webs between the fingers. They saw that both bodies were fingerprinted, and they collected and submitted the clothes as evidence. They rechecked the suspect's pockets, again finding them empty, and they made sure Charles Greene's valuables would be returned to his mother, Sonia Greene.

The Detective and his partner learned the young ME had been wrong: The bullet did not miss the suspect's heart and nick his pulmonary aorta. It hit his heart. ("How poor a marksman did you say Charles Greene was?" the Detective asked his partner. "I'd say he was pretty good, and he still died.") They also enjoyed the dubious satisfaction of seeing the robber's stocking mask removed, his face revealed. Dubious satisfaction because they didn't recognize the guy and he betrayed no particular agony. Just a 40-something white male, surprised he was dying. The pathologist took photos, and so did the Detective and his partner. They could at least look at the photo database until the fingerprints were run for matching.

Throughout the following weeks, evidence accumulated slowly. The initial neighborhood canvass yielded nothing. The kids at the fast-food restaurant said they never had a minute to leave the restaurant while they were working, much less walk to The Country Store. They didn't see any man in a trench coat, certainly no man who looked as awful as that guy in the picture—wasn't he dead, anyway? The residents at the apartment building, the few willing to answer their doors around midnight, hadn't been to the store, had been watching television, had been out at the movies, they were so sorry.

Fingerprints on the evidence confirmed that Charles Greene fired the Luger while the suspect fired the 12-gauge shotgun. The prints showed that both the suspect and the victim had touched the counter, apparently reached far across the counter. "Bet he got that shotgun in the boy's face," the partner said. And both the victim's and the suspect's prints were found in the cash register and on the brown grocery bag, as if the suspect decided Charles Greene moved too slowly, as if he needed to hurry him. Only Charles's prints were found in the safe, and among the many prints on the front-door handles, the suspect's were found only on the outside handle.

The suspect's fingerprint card was sent to the city, state, and FBI simultaneously, but the Detective and his partner knew results would take time. Two days later, they returned to the apartment building—this time with a list of residents—and again went door to door, and this time their luck was good. A 15-year-old babysitter who didn't live in the building but was there the night of The Country Store shooting and was there again two days later confessed: "I left the baby here alone and went across the street for a Coke. It just took a minute, and the baby was asleep, so I didn't think it would matter. When I left the store, a man in a coat climbed out of a car, and I noticed that—a coat when it was so hot." They asked if she saw the man's face, but she said no, he was still leaning into the car when she left. They asked her to describe the car and all she could say was it was white or maybe yellow, two- or maybe four-door. "The sort of car attorneys drive. That's what my mother says when she sees them. I thought of my mother when I saw the car, maybe because a woman was driving. I thought maybe she had very powerful air conditioning, that's why the man wore the coat."

"And you're sure of the time?" the Detective asked.

"Well, yeah," the girl said. "I left the Swansons' at 10:00 because they said they'd call at 10:15. I had to be back."

At the very least, the Detective and his partner could picture the entire crime. The robber waited until the store emptied, walked in, and displayed his shotgun, asking for the money in the register. Charles Greene began to put the cash in the grocery bag, but the suspect leaned over the counter and helped him, perhaps then spying the safe. He asked for the cash from the safe, and Charles Greene opened the safe and gave it to him. The suspect began to walk away, but Charles had found the gun his uncle kept there. He fired once and hit the suspect in the back, fired again and hit the pastry case. He fired a third time, but the suspect had already spun and lifted his shotgun, had already squeezed his trigger.

The city returned no fingerprint match, but the state and the FBI did. Their suspect's prints matched those of Nelson Fitz Smith, who had a long record of old-economy crimes: hold-ups, bank robberies, strong-arm robberies. The man had only been out of prison nine months for his last conviction. The Detective called Smith's parole officer, who gave him Smith's last known address (Smith had been in violation of parole for months), and the Detective and his partner drove to that address. It was Smith's mother's home, a three-story triple-family row house. The partner pointed out the "attorney's car," a creamy white Beamer parked at the curb. The Detective had two jobs. One was to find out who might have been driving Mrs. Smith's car on the night in question. The other was to tell Mrs. Smith her son was dead. The Detective hoped Nelson was an apple who fell far from his mother's tree. And what if Nelson and his mother were the same breed? Maybe the Detective would get the satisfaction of arresting her. But when he and his partner climbed the stairs to the third-floor apartment, they found the door unlocked, the apartment vacated.

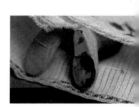

"She's someone's mother," the uniformed officer said. Weren't half the victims they dealt with? But the Detective knew what the young officer meant. He hated to think of his own mother, who was much older than this woman, lying cold on the kitchen floor. From the looks of it, this woman had been lying there for hours. It was way past dark: 10:57 p.m. on a cool September night—time for television, reading lamps, and nightlights, not glaring overhead kitchen lights. This overhead light shone too brightly on the unfinished cup of coffee and the two slices of toast, each with a bite or two missing, the morning edition of the paper propped up on the table at just the right angle for reading.

"Guess we're lucky the place didn't burn down," the Detective said, nodding toward the frying pan on the stove, a breakfast of sausage and eggs sunny-side up sitting untouched.

"One of the strange things we found," the officer said. "Someone had turned off the stove."

"The place was unlocked?"

"Exactly right," the officer said. "We responded to the daughter's call at 9:44 p.m. by walking around the perimeter, peering in the windows. We didn't see anything unusual until we got to this room, the kitchen. We could see Mrs. Washington lying on the floor." The Detective glanced at him, and the officer added, "We could see her with our flashlights on. We tried the door, and it was unlocked."

"So the door wasn't hanging open?"

The Detective was standing in the doorway, so it was hanging open now.

"No, it wasn't."

"And you wrote in your notes that you turned on the overhead light?"

Startled, the officer pulled out his notepad and said, "Yes, we did."

The Detective grunted. At times, it was worth it to be overbearing. He shook his head and said more gently, "There's a cake—looks like a fresh-baked cake."

"No cake pans in the sink," the officer said. "No bowl for the batter or whatever."

The Detective winked at the officer, still young enough so that everything about him looked fresh-pressed and crisp, not just his uniform. "Only someone who liked to lick the bowl would notice that."

The officer flinched, as if uncertain whether he was being made fun of, so the Detective said, "Yeah, I used to like to lick the cake bowl, too." He added, "You're absolutely right. Whenever Hazel Washington baked the cake, she cleaned up after herself and put everything away."

"So what do you think happened?" the uniformed officer asked.

"I don't know," the Detective said. "I just got here."

"There's a wound to her head."

The Detective nodded. Hazel Washington had taken a blow to the left side of her head. She had a small gash that had bled, though the blood had long since coagulated.

"Do you think someone hit her?" the Detective asked.

"Door's unlocked. Stove's turned off. And she's got a blow to the head," the uniformed officer said. "It seems possible."

The Detective bobbed his head as if he agreed, but he said, "There's not much blood, is there?" He squatted close to the

victim. "I don't think it dripped to the floor, and the wound is small." He scanned the placid room. "There's very little sign of struggle—one fallen woman, one fallen chair, a phone off the hook."

The Detective stood up and gazed about the room again, a normal room where a normal life had stopped, just like that. He spied something on the counter and asked, "What's this, by the toaster?"

"A syringe," the young officer said. "It's empty."

His hands already gloved (they had been since he climbed from his car), the Detective crossed the room and picked the thing up by its edges, mindful not to destroy latent prints.

"Hazel Washington does not do drugs," the Detective said flatly, "so I'll bet this is…." Gripping the thing by its striated cap, he picked up a small bottle, almost a vial, lying next to the syringe and read the label, "Insulin."

"I knew that," the uniformed officer said.

The Detective smiled to himself and returned both items to the positions in which he'd found them. "Well, if she was diabetic, which we don't know, she would have taken her insulin shortly before eating."

"Is that when they do it?" the young officer asked.

"I think so," the Detective said. Then he took a step back, as if fearing contamination, and added, "There's blood here on the counter."

"Do you think she fell?" the uniformed officer asked.

"And hit her head on the counter?" the Detective said. "I think that's possible."

The Detective looked at the receiver dangling against the wall. "At least the phone isn't buzzing at us."

"Must have stopped doing that hours ago," the officer said.

"Used to be," the Detective said, "they'd buzz at you until you hung them up again."

He left the receiver hanging. "So tell me again about the daughter."

"Like I said, she called the precinct at 9:44 p.m.," the officer said.

"Her name is?"

The Detective opened his notebook, ready to write.

The uniformed officer pulled out his notebook and flipped through the pages. "Sarah. Sarah Oates. That's O-A-T-E-S. Sarah Washington Oates. Her number is…" and the uniformed officer ticked off a 914 number.

"And what did she say?"

"She said that she had been trying to reach her mother all day long, and every time she called she got a busy signal." The uniformed officer gestured a *now we know* toward the dangling receiver. "Since her mother lives alone, she got worried. So finally, before it got too late, she called the precinct, asking us to check on her mother because Sarah lives a long plane ride away."

The Detective scribbled for a few moments, then asked, "Did she say how many times she tried calling her mother?"

"A lot—she tried calling her a lot." The officer looked at his notes. "Five times."

"It was her habit to call her mother?"

"I don't know," the uniformed officer said.

"Do we know how old the victim is?"

"No, we didn't get that information."

"Well, all right then."

"I mean, it's obvious we should have asked. I don't know why we didn't."

"That's all right." The Detective waved the worry away. "I can ask her later."

He dug out his cell phone and placed two calls: one to the ME's office and one to the mobile crime laboratory unit, asking for an evidence technician. He folded the phone away, all the preliminary steps taken care of. Only thing left was securing the site. The Detective winced and scratched his neck. It would kill him to put up CRIME SCENE tape at this poor woman's house if there was no crime. When he arrived, there'd been the usual crowd out by the black-and-white, attracted by the rhythm of the flashing lights. Stringing up CRIME SCENE tape would be like throwing chum off a boat— sure to make the seagulls clamor. But until he knew it wasn't a crime scene, he had no choice but to treat it as one.

He said to the officer, "I guess we better secure the site."

The uniformed officer nodded but took no action.

So the Detective said, "We need to secure the crime scene." And when that still didn't work, he said, "Secure the crime scene, officer. Get the tape out of your trunk and establish a perimeter."

"Right," the officer said, and then, "right, right," as if understanding he'd been given an order. "My partner and I can manage that," and he rushed out of Hazel Washington's kitchen.

One thing the Detective would say about working with fresh recruits, it made being boss of the scene easier. It might have made him feel old, but it brought home that he knew a thing or two, even if he couldn't recite *The Criminal Investigation Handbook.*

The Detective walked about the room, laying the lightest possible finger here or there. He used a different finger for each touch. He pressed a knuckle against the toast and found it cold. He dipped his pinkie into the coffee cup and found it cold, too. He lay the back of his hand against the coffee pot, and it was cold. Sausage, eggs, pan, and four burners, all cold. Even the fat in the pan had long since congealed.

He rolled off his gloves and labeled them, slipped on a new pair, then knelt down by Hazel Washington. Her lips had gone very dark, a long time cyanotic, he figured. He also noted the lividity of her skin, the deep purple that indicated the blood was starved for oxygen. Perhaps the uniformed officer was right. Perhaps she fell. Or maybe she died of asphyxiation. Maybe she choked. She was lying in a kitchen. Half-eaten food lay on the table.

The Detective pressed himself up from the floor, the way he did when his knee was bothering him, and slipped his cell phone from his jacket pocket. He flipped open his notebook and found the daughter's number. It was after 11:00 p.m. in Shadytown and would be 2-something in the morning where he was calling, an unholy hour for such a call. He wished the daughter didn't live so far away, so he could talk to her face-to-face. But she was hours away by plane, and he would have to tell her on the phone. The Detective almost hoped the woman wouldn't pick up, but she did. He identified himself and asked to speak to Sarah Oates, Sarah Washington Oates.

"This is she," she said quietly, as if he had awakened her. "What's happened?"

"I'm afraid I have to tell you your mother has died."

"Oh," she said, and nothing else for a long moment. "Oh God. I kept telling myself it couldn't be. It just couldn't be. How did you find her?"

He explained what the uniformed officers had found when they responded to her call.

"So why are you there?" Sarah Oates asked. "What happened that they need a detective?"

"Whenever someone dies unexpectedly," the Detective said, "we investigate the death. We treat it as…" Sarah Oates would have to face these possibilities at some time—perhaps the time was now—as a homicide or suicide until our investigation proves it isn't. I'm sorry to have to tell you this. Do you understand?"

"My mother never would have committed suicide."

"I'm sure she wouldn't have, ma'am."

He heard himself and shook his head. How rarely he had reason to say ma'am.

"Do you think someone *killed* her?"

"At the moment, I can't say. I hope the investigation will prove otherwise." He heard that too and tried to change it. "No, I don't believe someone killed her. But what I believe doesn't matter. It's my job to find out just why your mother died."

"Oh," Sarah Oates said. "Oh God."

The Detective waited, aware that the refrigerator had just hummed on and the kitchen clock was ticking away. When he thought Sarah Oates had regained her composure, he said, "It would help us if you could answer some questions. Do you mind if I ask a few?"

"No," she said quietly.

He waited to see if she meant *not ever*.

"No, I don't mind," she said.

Because he wanted to understand the presence of the insulin and the syringe, he asked, "Is your mother under a doctor's care?"

"More like she's under an HMO's care," Sarah Oates said. "But yes, she has a doctor, a primary care physician, I think it's called now. And he's not bad."

He asked for the doctor's name and phone number, and while she searched for them, he looked out the window.

Where it was situated, he couldn't see the ruckus on the street, the police car and the neighbors. The only sign he could see was the glow of the lights, flashing one after another: white-red, red-red-white. He could make out the neighbor's house, its pitched roof and backyard fence, the garbage cans huddled by the garage.

"Here it is," she said and gave him the information, which he in turn would give to the pathologist.

"Was she being treated for anything special?"

"First, she has diabetes," Sarah Oates said. "Insulin-dependent diabetes. She's had it since she was a teenager. I think they call it mature onset of diabetes of youth."

"Does your mother take insulin?"

"She does," she said. "She did."

"Had your mother been depressed?"

"Are you standing in my mother's kitchen?" Sarah Oates asked indignantly.

"I am."

"Does that look like the kitchen of a depressed person?"

He surveyed the room again, with its spotless sink and fresh-starched curtains, and realized he had no idea, no idea at all. He said, "I'm sure it's not."

He waited for decency's sake, then asked, "Did your mother live alone here?"

"She did," Sarah Oates said. "My mother has lived alone—without a husband—since I was a girl. We've been managing her diabetes since I was 10."

The Detective scratched his neck, asking himself what was appropriate to say. He settled on, "That must have been difficult."

"Yes, it was," she said. "It surely was."

"How old was your mother?"

"She is, she was 59."

"Not old," he said, for he wasn't *that* much younger.

"Not that old," she agreed.

"So she lived alone and she had diabetes," the Detective repeated. "Did anyone visit your mother regularly—a health-care worker, for instance?"

"No, she's far from incapacitated. She doesn't need a visiting nurse."

"So there's no one who came to the house regularly? No one who might come and go unnoticed?"

"No one I hired, that's for sure."

"Okay, so she lives alone and is completely independent," the Detective said. "Is this her own home?"

"Well no, it isn't," Sarah Oates said. "It's mine."

"You own her home?" He hated to repeat things, but it gave him time to write the answers down.

"Several years ago, she'd fallen behind on her mortgage, so I bought the house for her."

"The house is in your name?"

"That's right."

He could hear that she was wide awake now. "Who would her closest friend or relative be?"

"Well, I am, and I'll be flying out as soon as I speak to my boss."

"But until then?"

"That would be Rose," Sarah Oates said. "Rose Cooper. My mother's at 423 Country Road. Rose is at 587."

He wrote the information down and read it back to Sarah Oates, then said, "This may sound like an odd question, but does your mother subscribe to the paper?"

"She always did, and I suppose she still does."

"Does she have the paper delivered?"

"I have to answer the same way. She used to, and she must still. Why?"

"I mentioned the door was unlocked when the officers arrived, didn't I? That's good, because it was easy for them to get in, but it's not quite ordinary. I'm trying to find out why it was unlocked. Did someone have access to the house, or did she step out and pick up her paper and forget to lock it after her?" On impulse, he asked, "What time does your mother get up in the morning?"

"She works three days a week for the county. So most days, she gets up around 7:00, sometimes earlier."

"Do you know her routine?"

"She likes her breakfast, so if she's not going in to the office or she has the time, she makes herself some breakfast—bacon and eggs, sausage and eggs. If she doesn't have time, she just makes coffee."

"Does she do anything else?"

"She likes to read the paper—get her morning news."

It sounded as if Hazel Washington had been enjoying her typical morning.

Suspecting he had worn out his welcome with Sarah Oates, the Detective said, "Before I go, I'd like to hear about the phone calls."

"I call her two to three times a week. Because of the time difference, I often call her as soon as I'm awake enough, 6:00 or 6:30 a.m. my time, 9:00 or 9:30 a.m. hers. I called about then yesterday and got a busy signal. I called again when I got to work and got a busy signal again.

I called between meetings and got a busy signal. I must have called five or six times, and finally at supper, my husband and I discussed it, and I decided to call you," she said. "Or not you. The precinct."

"Since you were getting this busy signal," the Detective asked, "did you call the telephone company and ask them to check the line?"

"I asked my secretary to do that," Sarah Oates said. "And believe me, that was not easy—not even for a secretary as persistent as mine. Before he left, he told me he'd contacted what he hoped was the right company. They said there was no trouble on the line. They said perhaps the phone wasn't sitting quite right in its cradle, or that's what my secretary told me."

"Look, I am so sorry for your loss, Mrs. Oates," the Detective said. "I appreciate your patience." He gave her his phone numbers so she would know how to reach him once she arrived. "I'm sure the morgue will release your mother's body tomorrow morning."

"Are you telling me there's a chance they won't?"

"Yes, Mrs. Oates, there's always a chance."

The Detective was surprised the ME hadn't arrived yet. The Detective had started his shift at 4:00 p.m. that day, and until now, the day had been quiet. His partner was out with the flu, so the few new cases had been assigned to other teams. Until the call for this case came in, he had spent the day clearing out his inbox and finishing up the paperwork on all but closed cases. He couldn't imagine he'd have to wait for an ME, though it had happened before. He slipped out his cell to place another call, and while he was waiting for the phone to find a satellite, the evidence technician knocked. It was a tech he liked and had worked with before—a tech some of the detectives called "the mole." He was small, his eyes narrow-set, his brows crashed together on the blade of his nose. He worked quietly and intensely, for which he was also well known.

"I need to take photos straight away," the evidence technician said.

"I'm in your way," the Detective said.

"You will be."

"That's fine. I need to canvass the neighborhood."

The Detective walked down the path where the two uniformed officers stood on the sidewalk. CRIME SCENE tape now established a perimeter around Hazel Washington's home, and the uniformed officers made sure no one crossed the line. The lights on the squad car still flashed in sequence—white-red, red-red-white—and neighbors still stood about in their robes or their sweat suits or their jeans and sweaters. The Detective picked a man who might pass for observant, a man not chatting with his neighbors but standing alone in his old cords and slippers, sucking on a pipe. The Detective identified himself and asked the man his name and where he lived (directly across the street), then asked him to offer a few more particulars in case the Detective had reason to contact him again. To his surprise, the Detective asked a question he hadn't planned, "Do you know what happened?"

"Do I know?" the man said, pulling his pipe from his mouth. "I thought *you* were supposed to know that. I don't *know* anything. But I *heard* Hazel passed away unexpectedly."

The Detective said nothing, and the man continued, "I *heard* you came because her daughter called, worried—her daughter who lives *thousands* of miles away. I *heard* you found the kitchen door unlocked."

"How do you know Hazel?"

"Hazel and I raised our children here together," the man said. "My wife and I and our three children lived in the house across the street, and Hazel with her one daughter lived over here."

"Are you good friends?" The Detective wanted to know if anyone else could have entered that house, if anyone could have meddled with the victim's medication, and a good friend might know that.

"I'm a widower, and Hazel's been divorced as long as I've known her," the man said. "We socialize together from time to time. She was going to celebrate my birthday with me tomorrow."

"Your birthday's tomorrow? Congratulations," the Detective said. "I bet you're turning 55."

The man smiled and said, "You're flattering me. You know, I'm 70, going to be 71 tomorrow."

The Detective shook his head and said he didn't know, then resumed his questioning. "As far as you know, there was no one who came regularly into Hazel Washington's home?"

The man shook his head. "And that woman had *no* enemies."

"She wasn't depressed?"

"If she was, she hid it well."

"And you didn't see anyone entering or leaving her house this morning?"

"No, I didn't." The man drew on his pipe, then added, "She was going to bake me a cake."

"Was she?"

"For my birthday, as I said. She was going to bake, and I was going to cook the dinner."

For a moment the Detective thought the man might cry, so he waited until he could ask, "Do you subscribe to the paper?"

The man nodded. "Get it delivered every day. A nice boy puts it right on my doorstep."

"What time is it delivered on this block?"

"Around 5:30 in the morning."

"What time was it delivered this morning?"

"As far as I know, same time as usual," the man said. "I go out about 6:00 to pick mine up."

The Detective made a note, then thanked the man for his time, asking one last question before he moved on. "Do you know Rose, Rose Cooper?"

"I do," the man said, "but she's not out here. She lives in the 500 block, and I don't believe she knows yet."

The Detective had thought this man and Rose Cooper might console each other, but it wasn't his place to offer such suggestions, so he winced and smiled and moved on to the next interview. The answers he received from each interviewee corroborated each other. The paper arrived daily at 5:30 a.m., Hazel Washington had no enemies, and no one had regular access to her home. She was never depressed and always kind, her reputation as spotless as her house. She did like a good breakfast. She could bake a great cake. The only discrepancy came from a Mrs. Grant, a tall, outsized woman who knew Hazel Washington best from choir.

"That woman had a voice with wings," Mrs. Grant said. "We missed her at rehearsal last night. Had she not made it to Thursday's rehearsal, we would have been very worried. Well, by then, everyone would have known anyway. The papers would have piled up. The sad and funny part is we take turns bringing after-rehearsal goodies, and she was supposed to bring the dessert last night. She'd promised us her famous chocolate cake."

The ME—the one the Detective thought of as the country doctor—had arrived while the Detective was interviewing the bystanders. As the evidence technician worked quietly in the background, carefully wrapping, labeling, and bagging all the small articles left from Hazel Washington's last morning, the ME squatted by the victim's body and gave his preliminary report to the Detective.

"Well first, you've got to see the deep purple lividity. That's a sign of either asphyxia or heart failure. We won't know which until the autopsy. Given she's in a kitchen, it's tempting to assume she choked." He nodded toward the food on the table and in the frying pan. "Second, she's been here a good, long time—well over 12 hours and going on 18. No one's moved her, I can tell you that." He pointed to her neck, the parts of her arms that did not touch the floor, and the area behind her ankles. "You can see the blood has pooled and the skin's discolored—permanently." The ME shrugged gently, recognizing that nothing was permanent for the state of

the victim now, if it ever was. "The blood's clotted, and if I press it"—which he did—"it doesn't move." He waved the Detective closer. "You'll get a better look at the autopsy, but wherever her body did touch the floor is discolored the other way. It's light because the pressure pressed the blood away."

"Can you tell me anything about the diabetes? About the insulin?"

"Looks to me like she took her pre-breakfast med, the insulin she needed to move the sugar around for that meal. More than that I can't say."

"What about...what do they call it? Insulin shock?"

"You'll have to ask the pathologist."

"Could she have gotten a bum batch of insulin—something too strong or too weak?"

"Again, that's up to the pathologist and the crime lab when they check out the syringe and bottle."

"Here's my problem," the Detective said. "I can buy that she was eating something and choked. Since the sausage and eggs and the cake, for that matter, are untouched, she must have been eating toast. I believe that's what the pathologist will find. But she's choking and she manages to turn off the stove?"

"Maybe she couldn't walk and chew at the same time," the ME offered. "Maybe she walked to the stove and turned off the burner. Maybe she swallowed too quickly, choked, and tried to call 911."

"That's certainly one way it could have happened," the Detective said.

"What's the other?"

"Maybe something startled her," the Detective said. "Like the phone."

The evidence tech interrupted. "Will I be dusting for fingerprints?"

"Sure you will," the Detective said. "I'm not sure who we'll eliminate with elimination prints. We have no suspect whose prints would stand out from those of people who had so-called innocent access to this house. But of course we'll get prints."

"I was thinking," the tech said, "that when I'm done taking prints, you could hit redial on that phone and see what number comes up. If it's 9-1-1, you'll know that much."

The Detective agreed. "I'll know she didn't choke because she was rushing to answer the phone."

Before the autopsy began, the Detective gave the pathologist the phone number of Hazel Washington's doctor. Perhaps because the city's pathologist was calling him, the doctor picked up the phone immediately, and she was able to ask him detailed questions about Hazel Washington's history of diabetes and her treatment program. She wrote "neuropathy" and "control" on her pad, and once off the phone, explained that Hazel Washington sometimes had numb feet.

"And sometimes she had trouble controlling her blood sugar," the pathologist said. "That's why the daughter called so often. Otherwise, Hazel Washington was lucky. Her complications could have been far worse." She turned to the body. "Let's get started."

As the ME promised, the pathologist turned the body over and showed the Detective the victim's pressure points, all the bloodless spots where the body had rested. She also discovered the toast in the victim's throat, exactly as the ME and the evidence technician had expected. The pathologist ran a quick test for glycemic levels and found nothing surprising. The blood sugar was low, as would be expected if the victim had taken her insulin but not been able to eat her meal. Death might have caused insulin shock, but insulin shock didn't cause the death.

Blood typing and fingerprinting results both arrived about a day and a half later. The blood on the kitchen counter matched the victim's, which was no surprise. The surprise was that the only prints in the kitchen were Hazel Washington's. The Detective expected to find at least *some* belonging to someone else—Rose Cooper, for instance, or even Sarah Oates—but he didn't. Hazel must have washed every surface in that kitchen daily. He supposed that wasn't a sign of depression, but it must be a sign of something.

The toxicology report and chemical residue test results reached him about two weeks later. No poisons or traces of chemicals turned up in her blood, and nothing but insulin was identified in the syringe and bottle. No poisons or chemicals were found in her food—not in the coffee, the toast, the cake, or the sausage and eggs.

He wrote a complete report of the investigation and a simple report of the death: Hazel Washington died from asphyxia subsequent to choking on two bites of toast. He never learned whether Sarah Oates requested a copy of the report, and he never met her. She arranged for the funeral home to pick up the body from the morgue, and she never called. Because he wouldn't be a detective if he were not curious, he drove past Hazel Washington's house from time to time. Once he saw the man from across the street and stopped to speak to him.

"The house?" the man said, removing his pipe from his mouth. "I *hear* Sarah cannot bring herself to sell it—not that she would ever tell me."

5. The Dorm

"Where would I feel comfortable talking about this?" The victim sat at an oak table in the Theta House kitchen, hurling the Detective's question back at him. She was short but sturdily built, and her sandy blond hair seemed to have been pulled back hastily, her part ragged and haphazard. She wore a pink seersucker robe over a red tee-shirt (a camisole, his wife would have told the Detective) and dark jersey shorts, the Shadytown State University seal printed on the right leg. The victim glanced warily at the Detective, then pulled her cup close and circled it with both hands, refusing to look up at him.

Getting the message loud and clear, the Detective took a seat at the table. It didn't do any good to tower over her, nor to sit directly across from her, as if in a confrontation. So he chose the chair cattycorner to her, so she could look at him if she wanted, but was not forced to. "We can stay here," he said, "or we can sit in the living room, or on the porch. Anywhere you'd feel safe."

"Nowhere," she said quietly. "That's where I'd feel safe." And she began to weep, not loudly or hysterically, but steadily. It was the way she would weep throughout the interviews the detectives had to conduct, softly and without warning and ceasing for no reason the Detective could see. He cast his partner a look, but the man had already found a box of Kleenex on the counter and was setting it on the table. The Detective pulled out two and handed them to the girl. *Girl.* She was a young woman, aged 21, the uniformed officer had told him. At that age, the Detective's own daughter wouldn't have let him call her a girl, though that is the way he thought of her still.

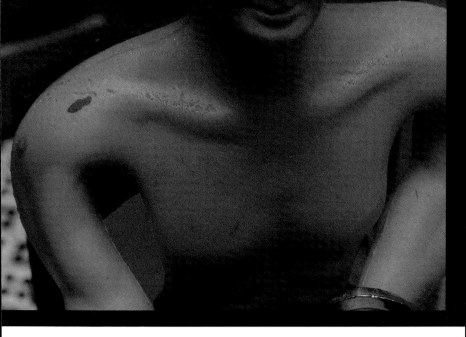

"This must be difficult," the Detective said.

The girl wept breathlessly a moment, then nodded. "It is."

"If you'd feel better," the Detective said, "we can arrange for a woman to interview you."

The girl exhaled audibly, not quite a gasp, not a sob. "But you're here. You're here now."

The Detective thought he understood what she meant: When the flood is rising, any rowboat will do.

"We may even seem like dull guys," he said, "asking sort of the same questions over and over."

The girl's face crumpled, and the Detective thought she would cry again, but she composed herself. "No, I don't think that. I don't think you're dull."

"That's good," he said. Though he had to cover some of the same ground the uniformed officer had covered, he intended *not* to repeat the questions. Still, he knew it could feel repetitious to the victim. "We just have to get the chronology down. You'll have to bear with us. You don't mind my partner taking notes, do you?"

The victim said she didn't and the Detective proceeded. He knew, or thought he knew, some of the facts already. The uniformed officer had already told the Detective what he'd learned when he responded to the 911 call at 4:07 a.m. The girl, one Mary Campbell, had met a fellow student at a university hangout, the Rendezvous Inn—better known as the 'Vous. The guy, Jack Kelley, was a dark-haired white male, roughly five foot ten and of medium build. They'd left the 'Vous together around 1:00 a.m., picked up a pizza, and gone back to Kelley's dorm room. There, the suspect had, according to Mary Campbell, forced sex on her, against her will, and she had fled his room and run back to Theta House around 3:00 a.m. That's when the officer had called the station and spoken to the Detective—when he knew he had a possible felony rape on his hands.

"So how'd you meet this Jack Kelley?" the Detective asked.

Mary Campbell looked at him askance, as if registering for the first time that the uniformed officer had already spoken to the Detective. "He was talking to a friend of mine, a guy I knew from Organic, and he introduced us. The three of us talked a while, and then it was just the two of us talking, me and Jack Kelley. We were having a good time, and he told me he was a T.A. in Biochemistry, which I have to take next semester. He seemed nice."

"So you hung out with this guy, this Jack Kelley, at the 'Vous?" the Detective asked.

"Yeah," Mary said. "We had a few beers together."

When she said no more, the Detective asked, "So you left the 'Vous?"

"It was, like, 1 a.m.," she said. "I told him Saturday was a long day of studying for me. He said he had to work all day Saturday, so we both had to leave."

She paused and looked at the dregs in her cup. Cocoa, the

Detective thought. There were two other cups on the table, both containing the last few pinkish brown sips of cocoa. He guessed she'd sat at the table talking to her sorority sisters. Natural enough thing—her friends giving her hot chocolate or tea—but she could have washed evidence away, depending on the specific nature of the sexual assault.

"He asked me back to his place," she said, "and I said yes, I'd like to go to his room."

That was always a bit of a stickler when the woman knew her assailant, admitting she'd had some interest in him, admitting she'd *chosen* to go to the room or get in the car. He shot a glance at his partner, who nodded, then said, "You know, it doesn't change anything. An attack is an attack."

Mary Campbell shifted in her seat, as if she didn't quite agree, and cried for a few minutes. Once composed, she said, "We got a cheese pizza first. We bought four more beers, too."

"Yes."

"Well, we went to his room in Cecil Hall," she said. "Room 3. A double on the ground floor. Cecil's an undergrad hall, so I said, 'I thought you were a grad student? What are you doing living in undergrad housing?' And he said he was a resident assistant, and I said, 'This is an R.A.'s room?' and he said it was. Isn't it great, ha ha? I thought it was a crumby deal, so I said, 'My R.A. has a single, a suite all to herself,' and he said, 'Yeah, they really cheated me, didn't they?' But then he said, 'It's okay. I like the perks.' I wasn't sure what that meant. I mean, Cecil is a coed dorm. I said, 'What do you mean?' But then we were talking about Beck and Björk, and I was telling him about the virology class I'm taking this summer."

"You ate the pizza?"

"I ate half a slice," Mary Campbell said. "I drank some beer, one or one and a half cans he poured for me into a glass mug. He drank the rest. I was starving. I'd gone running before I went to the 'Vous, but I'm on a diet and tried not to eat a whole slice or drink too much beer."

"So tell me how it happened," he said.

"He talked a lot," Mary Campbell said. "He told me he was going to go to medical school, and he talked a lot about being a T.A., first he said for Microbiology and then he said Molecular. He told me he was a National Merit Finalist and received a President's award. He asked me about being in a sorority. He said, 'That's pretty uptown, isn't it? So, are you one of those stuck-up girls?'"

"You don't look stuckup to me," the Detective said, hoping Mary Campbell would keep talking, and she did.

"He put some moves on me. We kissed some, you know, and he was kind of nice about it. Nothing too…pushy. I mean, he was saying these kind of mean things, like he wanted to prove how ignorant I am. He said something in Latin, and he was right. I don't know Latin. He laughed at me. 'Not that smart, are you, sorority girl?' But then he kissed me."

She paused and the Detective waited.

"I left something out before."

"That's okay," the Detective said, catching his partner's eye. Sometimes these interviews pivoted, the victim walking directly away from her accusation. Could be this interview was taking a U-turn.

"When he asked me to come back to his room, he kissed me," Mary Campbell said. "It was an A+ kiss, you know? I thought he was sexy before, and I really thought so then."

"What are you saying?" the Detective asked.

"That he wasn't who I thought he was," she said. "I got to his room, and I couldn't believe anything he said. I didn't believe he was a Micro T.A., and I sure didn't think he was a resident assistant. After a while, I told him I had to get going, or I'd be a mess trying to study the next…trying to study today. He didn't like that. He said, 'You got to study to get those MCATs up, sorority girl?' It was kind of mean, but I thought he was joking, so I tried to make a joke of it, too, like, yeah, I *do* have to study, I'm no Madame Curie. And that's when he did it."

"When he did what?"

"You know," she said, her hiccuppy weeping overcoming her. "He put one leg here." She pointed to one thigh. "And one here." She pointed to the other. "He grabbed both my hands over my head, with one of his." She stopped, as if she thought the rest should be clear, but the Detective remained silent and she continued. "Then he seemed mad because I was wearing shorts and underwear, and he had to push them off of me with his one hand and his feet. I asked what he was doing." Her voice grew shrill. "I swore and asked what he was doing and told him to stop. And then I started to cry. I was loud, I guess, because he put one hand over my mouth." Perhaps remembering what it felt like to have her mouth covered, perhaps remembering the intimation that she might never leave Jack Kelley's room in Cecil Hall, she broke down and cried for several minutes. When she recovered, she said, "I wish I'd bit him."

"But you didn't?"

A bite mark would be good proof the suspect attacked her.

"No, I didn't," she said. "But he had a hard time holding both my hands." She glanced away. "When he was, you know, touching himself. I'm pretty sure I scratched him then."

The Detective nodded, but said nothing, making a mental note to tell the physician or forensic nurse that Mary Campbell might have the suspect's blood or skin cells under her fingernails.

"He finished and rolled off of me, and I didn't even bother with the ladder. I sort of fell off his bunk, pulled on my shorts, and ran back here. Sort of. These sandals aren't the best for running. I swear I'll never wear them again. I can't believe I'm still wearing these clothes."

"This is what you were wearing? Not the robe, but these shorts and top?"

"Yes."

"Actually, it's a good thing you're still wearing the same clothes," he said. He couldn't tell Mary Campbell *she* was the crime scene. She was the site to be combed for evidence. So he said, "In cases like these, we have no witnesses. Sometimes, we have nothing more to go on than what you say. So we have to treat every trace of evidence left on you or your clothes very carefully. If there's some of him on those shorts, that's evidence. If you scratched him, maybe he left some of his blood or some of his skin cells under your nails. That's evidence. You understand what I'm getting at?"

"I do," she said, and he believed she did.

"I'm really sorry this happened," the Detective said, and he was. But the sorrier he was, the more he needed evidence—

some of which was sitting at the table with him in Theta House and some of which Jack Kelley could be destroying back at Cecil Hall. "I have to ask you some questions for clarification, and I have to explain to you about the medical exam at the hospital. But first, I have to ask you three difficult questions, all right?"

She looked scared, which was good, he figured. The questions couldn't be as frightening as the prospect of the questions.

"Did Jack Kelley ejaculate?" he asked, and though she shifted in her chair, she said yes.

"Have you cleaned yourself?" he asked, and she looked back, bewildered.

"Well, don't," he said. "For now, don't eat, don't drink, don't use the bathroom if you can help it, don't even wash your hands." Her hiccuppy crying resurfaced, and he said, "This is really hard, I know, but remember, we need every bit of evidence."

He asked when she'd last had intercourse, and she told him she and her boyfriend had broken up around mid-terms. "That means two or three months ago?" he asked, and Mary Campbell nodded.

He took the opportunity to tell Mary about the medical-legal examination that would have to be conducted at the hospital. She needed to understand that it would be thorough. The forensic nurse would collect seminal fluid and search for foreign hairs and fibers. The nurse would identify abrasions, bruising, and swelling, and she would take photographs to document those signs of trauma. The Detective explained that before the examination, either he or his partner needed to ask Mary about the specific acts committed, so the forensic nurse would know what to look for and where to look. He promised to give Mary a questionnaire, to make things easier on her. There would be one more detailed interview, he wanted her to know.

"So you understand why we don't want you eating or drinking or washing yourself?"

She said she did, and he told her he needed to ask her a few more questions—just to get a few more details. He wanted to know about the sandals. Did she stop to put them on afterwards?

"I never took them off. So no, I didn't stop for them. I didn't even stop for my underwear."

"So you left your underwear in Jack Kelley's room? You leave anything else?"

She looked back, bewildered. "I don't know. I really don't know if I did."

"Well, you went out to the 'Vous," the Detective said. "Did you take a purse or a backpack?"

"A purse," she said. "I took my purse. It's like a pink purse."

The Detective made a note to search Jack Kelley's room for Mary's belongings, her underwear and purse and anything else that might be hers. He asked her about falling down from the bunk, and she said that the top bunk was Jack Kelley's and that she'd climbed up the ladder with a glass of beer in her hand.

"A glass?" the Detective asked, and she said yes, a beer mug. Jack Kelley drank his beer from a can. "Prints," the Detective jotted in his notebook. He asked if she'd left the glass on the bed, and she said Jack Kelley took it from her and set it on the desk.

"There were no drugs?" the Detective asked. "No smoke? No blow?"

"*No.*"

"Far as you know, he didn't drug your beer?"

"Far as I know," she said, adding, "I didn't pass out."

"All right then, Mary," the Detective said. "Let me ask. Will you press criminal charges against Jack Kelley when we find him?"

The Detective thought he could see the questions forming: Trial? Parents? Publicity? All these questions again, and in public? But Mary said, "Yes."

The Detective looked at his partner, and his partner said, "I'm ready."

"Me too." To the victim, he said, "Mary, can you come with us?" and he explained what he needed her to do.

A brick building with white porticos, Cecil Hall looked distinguished from the outside, with pin oaks around the knoll and wrought-iron lamps along the walkways. But inside, the halls were painted dorm green and dorm beige; the doors were closely spaced, indicating narrow rooms; and almost every hollow door (such easy targets for break-ins, the Detective couldn't help but notice) doubled as nametag and bulletin board, announcing the character of the residents behind them. The Detective stopped outside # 3, which was decked out with a poster of a rap artist the Detective didn't recognize. In big letters stacked down the side, the poster read, "Ho, Ho, Ho." The Detective figured the guy wasn't quoting Santa Claus. The Detective turned to Mary, who for protection and moral support stood between his partner and the uniformed officer. Behind all three of them stood the campus security guard who had gotten them into the building. The Detective said, "Is this the room where you were raped?"

"Yes," she said.

He checked his watch (5:27 a.m.), then knocked on the dorm-room door. He thought he heard movement inside the room, so he knocked again and was considering his options—opening the door to prevent the suspect from destroying evidence or getting a warrant—when a shrubby-haired guy answered the door. "Are you Jack Kelley?"

The guy, who rubbed his eyes in a poor imitation of just awakening, said, "Yeah, I am. What's up?"

The Detective glanced back at the victim, who was paler than he'd seen her before. "Do you know this man?"

"Yes," she said. "That's the man who raped me."

The Detective said, "Okay, buddy," and his partner escorted Mary Campbell out of the building, while he and the uniformed officer herded Jack Kelley back into his room, the Detective saying, "We can come in, can't we?"

"You want me to stick around?" the security guard asked.

"You could wait out here," the Detective said. "Help us protect the crime scene until my investigators get here."

The security guard said, "Sure thing," and stood in front of the door, feet spread, hands on hips.

The uniformed officer cuffed Jack Kelley kindly, with his arms in front, while the Detective said, "You are under arrest for the rape of Mary Campbell," and read him his Miranda Rights: the right to remain silent; the right to consult a lawyer; the right to a lawyer free of charge. "Do you understand?"

"Of course I understand," Jack Kelley said testily.

The Detective appraised the suspect. The man was only half dressed, wearing dark slacks and black slippers with blue tassels, and his hair half-smoothed, as if he'd tried to make himself presentable. The Detective smelled no marijuana, but he did smell a potent aftershave. The suspect was fit, as if he spent most of his class time in the gym, and seemed closer to 25 than 18. Just when did children stop being forgivably rebellious teens and become intolerably arrogant adults?

"You may also answer questions, if you want," the Detective said. "You can choose to talk to us now without having a lawyer present."

"Why would I do that?"

The fact was the Detective had believed the victim's version of events, and he trusted his internal lie detector. He thought the *date* in *date rape* confused people, making it seem it was a matter of miscommunication: He said this and she said that, or she just changed her mind after the fact. But the Detective thought the *date* in *date rape* confused the *victim*. The rapist used the trappings of a date to disarm her, making the satisfaction of abusing the woman even sweeter for the man who was satisfied by abusing women. Mary Campbell had met a guy who brought her back to his room not for sex, but for rape. That's what the Detective believed. Yet, in the end, what he believed didn't matter. It didn't matter if he believed Mary Campbell set this guy up to avenge her wounded pride. What mattered was the truth and the evidence that led you to that truth. And what the suspect said might lead the Detective to other evidence. So he was not lying and he was not failing the victim when he said, "Because maybe from you I'll learn what really happened. Maybe I'll learn something that will clear everything up."

"Looks like you've already learned all you wanted to learn." Jack Kelley rattled the handcuffs.

"If you waive your right to a lawyer," the Detective answered, "you can always choose to stop answering questions, anytime you want, and wait to consult your lawyer."

"Yeah, right."

Getting irritated, the Detective turned his back on the suspect and slipped out his cell phone to call for evidence technicians. As he did so, he surveyed the suspect and the suspect's room, noting both the socks and the books on the floor, the discarded beer cans on the footlocker, the beer mug atop the desk, exactly where Mary Campbell said he'd find it. He told the evidence tech to get to Cecil Hall at State U. as fast as she could, then he slipped on a pair of latex gloves and pushed a chair under the suspect.

"So the nameplate outside said 'Jack Kelley' and 'William Jones'," the Detective said. "You already told me you're Jack Kelley. So who's William Jones?"

"My roommate."

"This is your room, then, the room you share with William Jones?"

"Yes."

"Where is your roommate? I mean, it's 5:30, 5:40 on a Saturday morning."

"He's away for the weekend."

The Detective gazed at the two bunk beds, which both looked slept in. "When did he leave?"

"Three days ago."

"He left Wednesday?" the Detective asked. "He's missing a lot of classes, isn't he?"

"He's not taking summer school. He's working, and they let him off for three days."

The Detective paced the room and slid one finger under the pizza. It was room temperature, the cheese congealed. He leaned close and squinted, but could make out no prints molded into the cool cheese. He rolled off the contaminated glove and labeled it, in case the evidence tech or any other investigator needed to examine it for residual evidence, then slipped a clean glove onto his hand.

"Do you know Mary Campbell?"

"Why wouldn't I know Mary?" the suspect said. "Everyone knows Mary."

The Detective gave the suspect a *good try* smile, both indulgent and skeptical. "Where did you meet her?"

"Where you meet..." The suspect paused, as if choosing his words.

"Where you meet what?" the Detective asked. *Victims?*

Whores? Easy prey? He wasn't sure he wanted to know how the suspect thought of them.

"Where you meet girls in this town. At the 'Vous."

"So when was that?"

"Around 10:30," the suspect said. "After all the real babes are already hooked up."

The Detective didn't say "I guess no real babe wanted to hook up with you?" because he wanted Jack Kelley to keep talking to him. He said, "Did you leave the bar with her?"

"I did," the suspect said. "I guess I shouldn't have."

"Did she come back here with you?"

The suspect leaned back in the chair, crossing his arms as much as the cuffs would allow, which wasn't much. "No. She didn't come back here. I walked her home."

"Where's that?" The Detective had continued to busy himself, reading the posters, examining the bulletin board, peering into the waste and laundry baskets, toeing the mess on the floor, the old newspaper, the socks, the books.

"Sorority Row," Jack Kelley said.

"The houses are pretty there," the Detective said. "Distinctive. Which one did you take her to?"

The suspect remained silent, and to prevent him from staying silent too long, the Detective asked, "So when did you get back to your room?"

"I don't know," Jack Kelley said. "Maybe 1:45."

"Did anyone see you return?"

"I don't know. We have card keys to the dorm. It's not like there's a security guard here."

The Detective leaned close to the suspect. "How old did you say you were?"

"I didn't. I'm 22. What of it?"

"What's your major?" The Detective had noticed the only textbook on the floor was a geology primer.

"I haven't declared yet."

"Kind of late, aren't you?"

"I took time off."

The Detective strolled back to the desk. "Since you got back from the 'Vous, has anyone else been in the room?"

"No," Jack Kelley said. "No one."

"But it looks like you had pizza with someone," the Detective said. "It looks like you drank one-two-three-four-five cans of beer, a lot of beer for a guy as fit as you." The Detective lifted one can by the rim, very carefully, and shook it gently to show that it was empty.

"Those are from, like, the entire week," the suspect said.

"Are they? Then I guess you're no Felix Unger. Hope William isn't either. You'd drive him crazy."

The suspect kept silent, the shadow of a smirk playing across his mouth.

"When did you buy the pizza?"

"I just got it. I woke up hungry and ordered it."

"The pizza place delivered it?"

"Yeah, they always deliver."

"Even though you have a card key and there's no front desk and no guard at the desk to let the pizza guy in?"

"Yeah, they call you, and you go to the door."

"Do they always deliver cold pizza?"

The suspect flinched. "It's been a while. I don't remember exactly when it came."

"But the pizza place will, won't they? They'll remember that you bought the pizza with a girl with blond, shoulder-length hair." The suspect said nothing, so the Detective asked, "Which bunk do you sleep in, Jack?"

"The bottom. The bottom bunk's mine."

"So why does the top bunk look such a mess?" the Detective asked. "Is that what you do when your roommate's away? Use the top bunk for girls and later sleep in the bottom?"

The suspect failed to remain blank-faced, the smirk lingering in his features.

Though the Detective would touch nothing that could be evidence, he could afford to be bolder now. "I see a pink purse in your wastebasket. How did that purse get there?"

Well, that wiped the smirk off the suspect's face, to borrow one of his mother's expressions. The Detective pulled the purse from the wastebasket, gripping it by the edges so he wouldn't disturb any prints. He slipped his hand inside and fished out a wallet, flipped it open with the lightest fingers he could manage, and saw the face of Mary Campbell smiling from her State University ID.

"So a pink purse containing Mary Campbell's ID just flew in through the window?"

The suspect said, "I haven't touched the trash. Maybe my roommate threw that purse in there."

"Your roommate?" the Detective said. "Your roommate who's been gone since Wednesday? Funny that Mary Campbell didn't report her purse missing two days ago."

The suspect swiveled away, and the Detective pressed ahead. "There seems to be blood on this towel here in your laundry basket. That's from the scratch on your arm, isn't it?" When the suspect didn't answer, the Detective said, "That's quite a scratch, isn't it? How'd you get it?" The silence continued, so the Detective reached out as if he might touch the suspect, saying, "Do you mind if I look at your arms?"

"Yeah, I mind," Jack Kelley said. "I don't want you touching me."

"Excuse *me*!" The Detective took a step back and feigned peering into the laundry basket again. "You know, I see a bit of pink lace in your laundry. Looks like girls' underwear to me, like undies. Whose undies are those? They're not yours, are they?"

"They're my girlfriend's."

"Who's your girlfriend?"

"Her name's Cindy."

"Cindy what?"

"Cindy Backstreet," the suspect said. "She doesn't go to State."

"But she left her underwear here?" the Detective said, as if deeply puzzled.

"She visited last week."

"She was here last week and her undies are on the top of the pile? I guess you wore the same clothes all week long?"

The suspect didn't respond, so the Detective crossed the room and opened a bureau drawer, rifling through the contents.

"That's not my drawer," Jack Kelley said, "and you can't search it. You don't have a warrant."

"I think you've been watching the wrong TV shows," the Detective said. "I can search this room incidental to your arrest."

"You're lying," the suspect said. "You've been tiptoeing around this room. I know you can't touch anything."

"You're almost right. I *won't* touch anything likely to be evidence, not before we've examined the room and documented it. But I can open this drawer. I can open your desk drawer." As he said this, the Detective opened the top desk drawer. With one finger he lifted the phone messages, library fine notices, and gym locker bills, and *Bingo*! discovered a baggie containing perhaps an ounce of weed, marijuana in his judgment. The Detective was almost embarrassed by his satisfaction. "When my evidence technician arrives," he said, "she will box and tag this bag of herbs, take it to the lab, and test it. And you will be charged with possession as well as rape."

"How'm I doing?" the security guard asked.

Though the Detective had just begun briefing the evidence technician, he stopped long enough to say, "Just swell," and he meant it. He'd kept the uniformed officer in the room throughout the suspect's arrest and interview, which meant there wasn't enough staff to string up the CRIME SCENE DO NOT CROSS tape, not until the evidence tech arrived. "Controlling the crime scene is 80% of the job." The Detective had no idea if that was true, but it conveyed that the job was crucial, and it satisfied the guard. The Detective thanked the man and told him he could return to his duties. "My partner and I will want to talk to your boss about the roommate. As long as this is a crime scene, we'll need to get a new lock for the door, and the roommate will have to get another room."

Through the open door of Room #3, the suspect watched the Detective, as if conjuring the evil eye. The Detective

wheeled around, saying, "And what do you think you're looking at?" As he resumed briefing the evidence tech, he stepped
out of the suspect's view, and so did the tech, a young
woman fresh from training. He knew her only as Milagros,
although now he could see her nameplate said *M. Real.* He
hadn't worked with her before, but her reputation—her
excellent reputation—preceded her. He'd already told her
about the purse in the trash, the marijuana in the desk drawer, the undies, and the bloody towel in the laundry.

"Can you shine an ultraviolet light on the bunks?"

"For sure," the tech said. "I'll be looking for blood, to confirm the victim's statement that she scratched him, and any
other bodily fluids. Later I'll go for hairs, fibers, and anything
else their bodies left behind. Maybe you want me to check
the roommate's bed, too, to confirm or refute the suspect's
statement that he was sleeping in the bottom bunk?"

The Detective didn't have time to agree because the tech
moved on. "I'll need elimination prints from the suspect and

the roommate, so we can distinguish the victim's prints from
theirs and substantiate that she was in the room. That means
we've got to get the victim's prints. Does she know that?"

"Not yet," the Detective admitted, and then they discussed
all the surfaces where they expected to find prints: the beer
cans, the pizza box, the doorknobs, the ladder, the beer glass,
plus any surface of the purse that might hold prints. The
Detective and the evidence tech both stepped under the tape
and into the room, where the suspect leaned back in his chair,
his eyes half-closed, as if he wouldn't deign to look at them.

The evidence technician pulled out her digital camera,
scanning the room, apparently deciding the best way to get
long shots and close-ups. The Detective told the uniformed
officer that he'd be taking the suspect down to the station. "I
need you to stick around and protect the crime scene, espe-

cially since students are starting to gather outside the door," the Detective said. "Be sure it's locked up when you leave. I'll be talking to Security and anyone else I have to about protecting our scene from intruders."

The tech held her camera high over her head and squeezed off several shots with her flash.

"Hey!" the suspect said, squinting as if the light was vinegar cast in his eyes.

"Don't worry," the Detective said to him. "We're getting you out of here." He assisted the man up, and with a hand on the back of the suspect's head, ducked him under the tape. The Detective was about to face down the phalanx of undergrads lining the hall—boys, for the most part (he decided this was the boys' floor), in tee-shirts and boxers and sweatpants—and walk the suspect down the hall when the evidence tech called after them. She held her camera out to the Detective, its viewing screen open for him to see.

"What have you got here?"

And then he saw what she had: Her random shots revealed a streak of blood on the top-bunk sheets.

"Thought you'd want to see that before you left," she said. "You're tall, but I didn't think you were tall enough to see this."

He checked to make sure the suspect could not see the photo, then said, "You should be able to get a good sample from that."

"Don't I know it."

The Detective took the suspect by the elbow and led him out of Cecil Hall, aware with every step of the undergrads saying, "Kell," and "Jackie boy," "Serious, dude," and "They got you this time."

Some cases closed with a gratifying click, secure as the latch of an old suitcase. When the Detective returned Mary's

purse the next day, he saw she wasn't doing well, which didn't surprise him. His partner had reported back after the medical–legal examination that despite the protection of the questionnaire—no detective asking personal questions, just an impersonal sheet of paper listing the clinical terms for a variety of sex acts—the victim had broken down recalling the details: that in his haste, the suspect had kept his pants on; that he'd gotten angry when he lost his erection and had to stroke himself; that he'd grown angry again when she was difficult to penetrate. After the examination, when the partner was conducting the final, detailed interview, she had stopped talking altogether and demanded to see the photos of her bruises. Mary didn't react to the photo of the bruise on her right wrist, perhaps because she could see it whenever she looked at her hands, perhaps because it was still a narrow red mark, like a rope burn.

But she turned away when shown photos of the fresh bruises on her thighs, and she was surprised by the bruises on her shin and right foot. "I don't remember getting these," she said. The partner had to say, "I think he kicked you. I think he kicked you as he pushed off your pants."

"He kicked me?" she said. "Like some dog?"

Residue from the fingernail scrapings of the victim's left hand proved to be the suspect's blood. The seminal fluid in the victim's vagina proved to be the suspect's, as did the stray pubic hairs combed from the victim's own and the stray hairs stuck to her tee-shirt and shorts. Inside, Mary's shorts were stained with semen, corroborating that she'd fled before she found her undies, and the semen also proved to come from the suspect. Mary never asked to see the Physical Examination report, so she never learned the forensic nurse indicated she was mildly intoxicated. She also never learned the nurse had remarked on the bruising and swelling all around the perineum.

Bit by bit the evidence collected from the suspect's room added to the picture. There was no question Mary had been in the room, for her fingerprints were everywhere: on the ladder, the beer mug, the beer cans, and all over the outside of the pizza box. No pizza boy delivered that box, unless the pizza boy was Mary. Semen on the sheets and bedspread was the suspect's, but sandy blond hairs found on the top-bunk pillow belonged to the victim. The pubic hair and vaginal secretions detected on the pink undies definitively came from Mary, while the suspect's underwear carried both the victim's secretions and his own semen. And the blood on the sheet and towel came from no one but the suspect. No question, the evidence looked bad for Jack Kelley.

The Detective and his partner canvassed Theta House, talking to the sorority sisters who had talked to Mary immediately after the incident and who would know best her first reactions. One girl said weepy; another said withdrawn; her roommate said shattered. None of them had seen Mary out with Jack Kelley before, and none saw him escort her home to Theta House that night.

The night manager of the pizza place had no difficulty identifying Mary and Jack. He said they came in around 1:10 a.m. Friday night, and the girl paid for the pizza and beer. But no matter how carefully the Detective and his partner scoured Cecil Hall, they could find no witnesses who saw the victim and suspect returning to the dorm, and none who saw the victim fleeing.

The partner summarized the case this way: "We've got two crime scenes, the room and the girl herself. The room evidence says the girl was there, and it says she had sex with the guy. It even says she got a little tipsy and forgot her undies and her purse. And it says she gouged the guy with her nails, but it doesn't exclude consensual sex. The evidence on the girl suggests rough handling, but does it prove rape?"

"The bruises say she was pinned to the bed," the Detective said. "You call that rough handling but not rape?"

The partner said, "I'm trying to account for the evidence."

"Account for this, buddy," the Detective said. "Everything the victim said turned out to be true. Nothing the suspect said has turned out true."

The following day, the Detective visited the Security office at Shadytown State University. He had to speak to the person in charge about William Jones, who had lodged a complaint about being displaced. While talking to the head about the importance of keeping the crime scene secure, the Detective recalled something the suspect had said: There were no security guards watching the doors. "If you don't have security guards watching the dorm doors," the Detective said, "you must have security cameras." Security not only had security cameras at every dorm entrance, it also saved the tapes. "Your tax dollars at work," the head of security said, though it took half a day to requisition the tape.

The Detective watched it alone first, then showed it to his partner. Two sequences—1:38:10 to 1:38:59 and 2:46:49 to 2:47:08—they watched repeatedly. In the first, Mary Campbell paused in the vestibule, the pizza box resting in her hands, until the suspect grabbed the box and then grabbed her wrist and dragged her in. In the second, a disheveled Mary Campbell ran through the vestibule, nearly slipping in her sandals and struggling with the heavy front door. The Detective and his partner watched these sequences over and over. Then they labeled the tape and marked it as evidence.

6. The Hotel

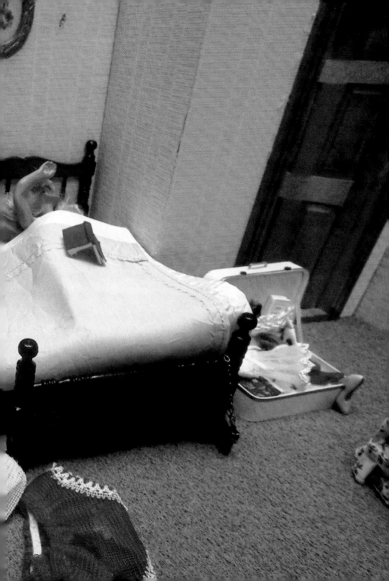

"We got the first call from the room above," the hotel security guard said, staring at the burnished elevator door, no doubt because that was the only surface that did not reflect his face back to him. "4-0-7. The guest said they heard a shot so loud they thought it would come through their floor."

Hotel security had taken its time greeting the Detective and his partner in the lobby, which seemed unusually active for nearly 8:00 p.m. on a Wednesday night. Two taxis were being loaded when the Detective and his partner pulled up, and the valet was bringing a family's SUV into the carport. The Detective watched the tall husband tipping the valet, the red-headed wife keeping the children near her on the verandah, wearing a face of false calm.

Suitcases sat in the lobby, and a short line of people was waiting at the reception desk. His knee had been bothering him, so while he waited for his partner to park the car, the Detective took a seat in the row of lobby chairs and flipped out his cell phone to call the ME, idly observing the departing guests. He could see clear through to the hotel restaurant, a place of local renown, the Riverbank, where a few diners—a very few—sat in a dimly glowing room. He watched a woman with bobbed hair curtly pay her bill and carry her bags out the door. He watched a man in a suit emerge from the men's lounge, cross the lobby, and take a seat next to the Detective, nestling a shopping bag at his feet. As taxis arrived, the guests vacated the chairs next to him one by one. First, one woman and then the other, and then the man sitting next to him stood, rattled his bag annoyingly, and left.

"Has 407 checked out?" the Detective asked. He avoided looking in the elevator mirrors. Why did decorators think mirrors disguised the fact you were enclosed in 128 cubic feet?

"No, he hasn't," security said. "But as you saw, several were checking out when you came in. Rumors have spread."

"It's not exactly a rumor," the Detective's partner said.

"It is when they use the 'M' word," security said.

"Murder's certainly a possibility when one woman's dead of a gunshot."

"Not *murder*," security said. The elevator doors opened then. "*Manson*. Now that's way out of the ballpark, you'll have to admit."

"You have any other incidents like this?" The Detective followed security down the hall, while his partner followed him.

"We're a hotel," security said. "We have our suicides. We've had our break-in rapes. Five years ago, we got a new security system for our emergency exit doors and established new rules for housekeeping and maintenance. Since then, we haven't had that kind of trouble, though we have had clients press charges against others. There was a famous murder here years ago. But in my time, we've had mostly theft—jewelry, laptops, expensive clothes. Bogus claims, a lot of them. We're choosy about our staff. And, we get our share of unexpected deaths. But we're normal. We compare favorably with national averages, as my boss says."

Even without the yellow CRIME SCENE DO NOT ENTER tape, the Detective and his partner recognized Room 307 from far down the hall; it was the room with the crowd fanned in front of it. The uniformed officers were busy taking statements from each person, but stopped when the Detective and his partner walked up with security.

The Detective said, "One of you should go ahead and get names and room numbers." One uniformed officer nodded at the other, who returned to notetaking. It was the female officer who said, "Excuse us!" to make the onlookers move and lifted the tape for the detectives to duck under. She gave security a cold stare, and he waited outside the room.

"So the call came in at 6:55 p.m.," she said, "and we got to Shadytown Bridge Inn at 7:13 p.m., got up to this room by 7:17. We knocked, but got no answer. We knocked and shook the door, but still no answer. In case evidence was being destroyed, we told security to open the door for us, and he did. We saw what you see—a woman with gunpowder all over her face, clothes on the floor, her hand clutched like that—and immediately I called you in, secured the room, and started to interview the people in the hall."

"What's her name?"

The officer opened her notebook. "Sally Johnson. She's an attorney, in town for some kind of legal business."

The Detective and his partner took in the disarray. No doubt the "M" word was an exaggeration, but that didn't mean much when they saw the torn nightgown and underwear lying on the floor, the clothes strewn haphazardly in the suitcase, the scar from a gunshot on the wall above the bed, the phone off the hook, the television dark and silent, the ice bucket on the bureau with what looked like a bottle of champagne, and two full glasses, a few bubbles still rising.

"Through all that," the partner said, "the clock/radio remained unfazed."

"They didn't even pull the plug," the Detective said.

"That thing was off?" the partner asked, indicating the television.

"No," the officer said. "I was just about to tell you that everything is as we found it, except that. The television was blaring when we arrived, and I turned it off."

"Carefully, I hope," the Detective said.

"Carefully as I could," the officer answered. "I couldn't find the remote. I couldn't leave it on, calling attention. It was the reason for the first call."

"I thought security said 407 called first, reporting a gunshot."

"Eight, nine minutes before that, 305 called because the TV in 307 was too loud—had been for 10 or 15 minutes. I took their statement."

"You learn anything else interesting from the statements?" the Detective asked.

"Sure," the officer said, and flipped open her notebook. "309, 306, and 407 all said they heard screaming, which at first they ignored. As the woman in 306 said, 'It wasn't like pain; it wasn't like childbirth'." The officer explained, "It stopped and started, like whoever was screaming couldn't decide whether to scream or not."

"Maybe she was too scared to scream—most people are if they've never seen a gun," the Detective said. "Or maybe she couldn't decide. Does screaming save her or kill her?"

"Or maybe she couldn't decide whether she's scared or having fun?" the partner said.

"Right," the Detective said. "Or maybe someone was stopping her from screaming."

"Whatever," the officer said. "Then the neighbors heard the first shot. They all claimed to know it was a gun. The guy in 309, he said he knew it wasn't a car backfiring since there weren't any cars on the third floor."

"Bright guy," the partner said.

"And that's when the woman really started to scream," the officer continued. "They all called the front desk, and then they heard the second shot."

"Guess all the incoming calls prevented the front desk from

finding out why Sally Johnson's phone was off the hook," the Detective said.

"I don't get this," the partner said. "Everybody's so concerned, yet they don't see anyone leaving 307?"

"They holed up in their rooms," the officer said. "Even 407, who was worried about gunfire coming through the floor. Only 306 admitted it, though."

The Detective and his partner circuited the room, one to the right and one to the left, mincing through the minefield of evidence.

"Ice in the bucket's partially melted," the Detective said.

"What are they?" the partner asked. "Square or round?"

"Square," the Detective said, and took a quick measure. "Melted, they're just under one inch by one inch."

"Remind me to check the ice machines later."

"Remind *me*," the Detective said. "Glasses seem to have the hotel monogram, SBI, as does the bucket."

"Underwear's plainly ripped," the partner said.

"Like the nightgown," the Detective said.

"Note the underwear is red and lacy," the partner said. "And the gown might be called lingerie."

"Note the champagne is uncorked," the Detective said. "And note one of the first things we do is talk to room service—find out if Sally Johnson even ordered champagne."

"Purse is hanging from the bedstead, unopened," the partner said. Touching only the edges, he opened the flap and pulled out a wallet, which he also opened. "And it is Sally Johnson's."

"Here's her checkbook," the Detective said. "Sally A. Johnson, 35829 Appletree Road—sitting right on top of her briefcase."

"This'll make you happy," the partner called, his voice in slight reverb. "Looks like a guy took a whiz in here."

"In the bathroom?" the Detective asked. "You said, 'A guy took a whiz'?"

"Seat's up," the partner said. "I don't think it's Sally Johnson's pee in here."

"At least we can get the murderer's blood type and DNA. Narrow down the field."

"You check the temperature of that bottle?" the partner asked.

"To see if it was chilled before it went into the ice?" the Detective asked.

The partner stretched his arms. Well, yeah!

"Excellent point, buddy, but I'd rather not destroy any good fingerprints."

"Whatever you say." The partner knelt by the suitcase and studied it as if he had X-ray vision that allowed him to see inside the folds of every garment, the corners of every pocket. "Think we'll find the guy's number tucked somewhere where her husband wouldn't find it?"

"What do you actually see, buddy?"

"Some kind of camisole or chemise," the partner said.

"Chemise?" the Detective said.

"That's what my girlfriend calls hers," the partner said. "And there are these pink heels, and toiletries in the pocket, plus a prescription bottle."

"Prescription for what?" the Detective asked.

The partner grasped the cap's grip edge, as it wouldn't offer prints anyway, and lifted it out. "Desloratadine? That mean anything to you?"

"It means it's not an antidepressant," the Detective said.

"Think there's any truth to what they say?" the partner asked. "These new drugs just make you well enough to kill yourself?"

"Doesn't matter in this case."

"Remember to ask the ME about side effects with this drug," the partner said.

"Now you're thinking," the Detective said, adding, "Window latch appears to be in place." He waited, as he always did when he disagreed with his partner, then said, "I just don't see this as a tryst gone sour, buddy."

"Whoever it was, he didn't crawl in the window to get here."

"Whoever it was," the Detective answered, "she didn't put the chainlatch on behind him. I mean, if it was your romantic hideaway, you would, wouldn't you?"

"Maybe, maybe not." His partner stood near the foot of the bed, stroking his tie and staring at the wall. "Is a bullet stuck in that gouge?"

"Looks that way from here," the Detective said. "Gun's lying nice and cozy under her right arm."

"What is it?"

"Looks to be a .38 Special."

"Good thing the guy didn't know she couldn't have shot it."

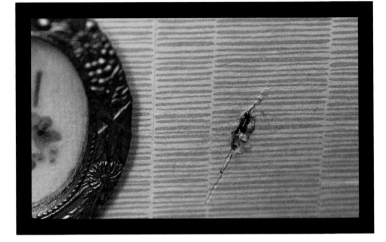

The Detective said, "I guess that's a good thing."

"Her hand and arm in that cadaveric spasm," the partner said. "How'd we end up inheriting that reaction? Why do people who die in agony die with their hands clutched? Too bad she didn't clutch part of our guy."

"Vicious tattoo on her face," the Detective said. Gunpowder—burnt, burning, and unburnt—had blown onto Sally Johnson's face, around the entry wound, the way gunpowder does when a weapon is within inches of its target. "Way it covers her face, I'd guess he held the gun a foot from her face."

"I'm telling you," the partner said, "my gut's screaming dangerous liaison—a pickup gone bad, a lover's quarrel."

"The only thing my gut screams is hunger. My head screams we got to look at the evidence."

"So you tell me," the partner said, "are you all tucked in by 6:55 p.m. when you're traveling?"

"You're saying she was in her nightie waiting for someone?"

His partner spread his hands. Well, duh!

"I'm saying the woman had a hard day doing what attorneys do—taking depositions or something. Maybe she had an early start tomorrow so she dropped anchor early."

"The ME's here." The partner lifted his chin toward the medical examiner investigator ducking under the tape. "When'd you call?"

"While you parked the car, buddy. A shot to the head? I knew it had to be an ME's case," the Detective said. He took another look at Sally Johnson, the pink bedding all pulled up around her. "The Bible's a nice touch."

"I can't believe the guy thought we'd buy it."

"You need me in here?" the officer asked.

The Detective appraised her a moment—hazel-eyed and sharp-featured—though he didn't need to. "We have to interview half the staff and all the guests, and we haven't gotten started. Ask your partner to take over securing the crime site. You take over interviewing the guests. Get all the basics: name, profession, address, purpose of trip, and then anything they know about the victim or the incident. How does that sound?"

"Sounds *good*," she said, as if *good* meant *great*.

"Hey," the ME said, "your evidence techs are on the way up. Thought you'd want to know."

The Detective had worked with this ME before, though he wasn't sure how she'd come to the profession. She wasn't an aspiring med student, that much he knew. Her version of professional included heels with pantsuits, as well as accuracy, care, and good judgment. She'd kept the job longer than most.

She said, "I'm not going to be able to tell you anything for a while. You know how I am."

"We know how to keep ourselves busy," the partner said.

The Detective stopped to give her a rundown of everything they thought they knew so far, and she wrote it all down. He turned back to his partner and as they left the room said, "You noticed there was no tray?"

"What?"

"No tray with a bud vase and a rose inside."

"Of course there's no tray," the partner said. "The room-service guy took it."

"Did he?"

"And this is the only order pad you use for room service?" the Detective asked.

"If we use more than one," the night manager of the Riverbank said, "we lose our orders. We use only one pad; it keeps everything simple. The maitre d' takes the orders until the restaurant closes. He punches them into the computer order system. They come up in the kitchen, and the staff prepares them, sets them out the back window, where the room-service wait staff loads them onto the trolley and sends them out."

"Same thing for drinks?"

"Same thing. Only difference is someone's got to take the drinks to the trolley. If the order is *drinks only*, then the bartender or maitre d' takes the drinks tray back to the window. If it's *with food*, the room-service waiter picks up the drinks once the meals hit the window."

"And no one ordered a bottle of champagne for Room 307?"

"Look at the checks for yourself."

The night manager handed the Detective the order pad. The Detective thumbed through it, seeing no order for champagne for any room. He also checked the numbers and saw no ticket missing from the sequence. "There's a log in the computer, too?"

"Sure," the night manager said, and clicked on the screen. "We really don't lose orders anymore. We used to, when the whole thing was done with carbons, but now nothing gets lost."

The Detective scrolled through the list. "Can you cancel an order?"

"Our system doesn't erase," the night manager said. "It marks the order 'Cancelled' or 'Changed'."

"I don't see any orders for champagne tonight," the Detective said. "You want to take a look, buddy?"

The partner gave the Detective a tossed-towel look. "All right. Where do you keep your champagne glasses? Your ice buckets?"

"All the glasses are by the bar." The night manager pointed to the overhead racks. "And the good ice buckets—not the plastic ones in every room, but the good ones we use for wine ordered with the meal—those are behind the waiters' bar station." He pointed to a cupboard near the bar, where water glasses were stacked and water pitchers sat sweating.

"And where do you keep your Veuve Clicquot?" the Detective asked.

"Is that what it was?" the partner asked, and glanced sharply at his superior.

The Detective shrugged, and the night manager said, "We have a special wine cellar for our most popular white and sparkling wines." He stepped around to the waiters' bar station and pointed to a wood-veneered refrigerator at the far end of the counter. "It's my job to lock it when we close, the day manager's to unlock it for lunch."

"Would you know if a bottle was missing?" the partner asked.

"This *is* a restaurant," the night manager said. "We control our inventory pretty well, but we can't do what department stores do, put sensor tags on everything."

"How about a list of what's in there now?" the Detective asked.

"Why not?" the night manager said, and spoke to the bartender.

The partner looked slantwise at the bartender and said, "Just be sure you can vouch for the list, okay?"

"Mind if we take a look at the room-service station?" the Detective asked.

"Not at all," the night manager said, and walked them down the corridor from the front of the Riverbank's kitchen to its back. The corridor ended in a T: Directly ahead was a coolly lit alcove for telephones and the men's and ladies' lounges, graced with a spare table and bare Manzanita branches in a lacquered vase; to the left was the open double doorway that led to the lobby and elevators; to the right was the room-service station and the swinging doors to the kitchen, locker room, and storage areas. Back kitchens and restaurant storage always had a certain smell, though the Detective couldn't place it—some mix of mold, mildew, and chemicals. He associated it with his mother's nursing shoes, those white shoes she always kept under the bed. She scrubbed them and polished them, but they always smelled of this odd, persistent smell. Through the long pass-through he could see men working—Mexicans, he thought, short, caramelized, sweating in the kitchen. They'd probably prefer to be called Chiapan or Guadalajaran, the Detective thought. They'd probably prefer to be called by their blasted names. They glanced at him furtively, it seemed, but he and his partner paid no mind. The night manager pointed out two room-service trolleys lined up under the window and a room-service waiter sitting in a chair against the wall. Past the trolleys, the Detective and his partner noticed stacks of green racks filled with dishes and glasses.

"What are those?" the Detective asked.

"Our clean dishes, ready to be stacked," the night manager said. "That's the busboy's job."

"How many room-service waiters you got?" the partner asked.

"Two on most nights," the night manager said. "Like tonight."

The Detective and his partner poked around, opening the doors to the lounges, the kitchen, the locker room, and storage rooms. They poked around, watching the busboys carry the green racks out front, until the second room-service waiter returned pushing an empty trolley. The Detective and his partner studied the man, then traded a look. Their guy didn't work this hard, that's what the Detective thought. Still, when he and his partner returned to the maitre d's desk and the night manager handed him the list of champagnes, the Detective said, "I don't want to alarm anyone who works here, but we're going to need a list of everyone working in the restaurant tonight—just in case we've got to clear each one."

"It's just for us," the partner added. "We've got nothing to do with Immigration."

"Everyone who works here has a valid green card," the night manager said.

The Detective eyed him. "You can't imagine how much we don't care."

He folded the champagne list and slipped it into his pocket.

Security looked over the shoulder of the front-desk clerk as she pulled up the information on Room 307. A young woman meticulously groomed—hair sprayed and barretted back, lips glossed, nails manicured and buffed—she seemed both eager to please and reluctant to hand over Sally Johnson's records. As the printer scrolled out the bill for Room 307, the clerk read from the computer screen.

"Sally A. Johnson checked in last night for a two-night stay," the clerk said. "She checked in at 7:17 p.m., and she requested early check-out tomorrow."

"How early?" the Detective asked.

"We just slip the bills under the door around 2:00 in the morning," the clerk said. "But let me look at something." She struck her keys rapidly and stared at the screen. "At 6:06 p.m., Room 307 requested a 3:00 a.m. wake-up call." The clerk tapped her keyboard again. "And she requested a seat on the 4:00 a.m. airport shuttle."

"Early flight," the partner said.

"Maybe not so early," the clerk said. "Not if she had to check in two hours in advance. A lot of our business travelers take the 4:00 airport shuttle."

The clerk handed the bill to the Detective, and he handed it to his partner.

"What time did your shift begin?" the Detective asked.

"This week I'm working the four to midnight shift," the clerk said.

"So did Sally Johnson speak to you before she went up to her room?"

"We have so many guests."

"Seventy-some rooms," the partner said. "That's not that many."

"My memory is, she paused to ask if she had messages. I checked our message center and told her no. We have voice mail, so we don't have many handwritten messages."

"Did she seem disappointed?" the partner asked.

The clerk shook her head slightly. "I think she asked out of habit—like she'd just walked in the office and was asking her secretary."

"And was she expecting anyone?" the partner asked.

"I wouldn't know." The clerk smiled benignly, a smile that made the Detective notice the plane of her cheek and the large faux pearl on her ear.

He said, "But you might know what time she came in?"

"Not long after I started."

"I guess that's about it." The Detective glanced down at his partner. "You have any questions about that bill, buddy?"

"Looks pretty straightforward." The partner ran a finger down the page. "We've got her business address and a contact at work. She didn't use the room phone at all, not even for local calls. Think her firm gives her a business cell?" When no one bothered to answer, he said, "She ordered no food last night, had a continental breakfast in her room at 7:30 this morning, and she charged her Riverbank meal to the room just a few hours ago."

The clerk winced and averted her face.

"Now that's something we didn't look into." The Detective waited a moment for the clerk to collect herself, then held out his hand for her to shake. "We thank you for your help."

When he saw the Detective and his partner coming, the Riverbank's maitre d' pulled two menus from behind his desk and said brightly, "Dinner for two?"

The Detective said, "You're joking, right? We need to see the manager again. We told him we'd be back."

Soon enough, the night manager walked briskly down the corridor, an envelope in his hand. He handed it to the Detective, saying confidentially, "Your list."

"That's great, that's great," the Detective said. "But it's funny how we overlooked the obvious, and you overlooked the obvious."

"What's obvious?" The night manager shrank ever so slightly inside his suit.

"You thought we meant you?" the Detective said. "No, I meant Room 307 charged her dinner in this room just four hours ago, and you didn't think to look it up, and we didn't think to either."

"Of course," the night manager said, then clicked into the maitre d's computer and scrolled through a screen or two. "Well, it's been slow tonight for the reasons you know, and it's always slow around 5:00. We sat Sally Johnson at Table 8. Silvia waited on her."

"Silvia's still here?" the partner asked, and the night manager pointed her out, tall and apparently pensive, leaning against a column in the Riverbank's dining room. "You can talk to her," the night manager said. "She's just waiting for her customers to finish their meals."

"We will," the Detective said, "but we'd also like to see Ms. Johnson's check." He paused and looked around the room, at the island of half-moon banquettes and the tables floating far apart, backed by a mural of a shady, tree-lined river, a bridge across it, and a white inn at the foot of the bridge. "You know, we should see all the checks for the night. Can you do that—get all the checks?"

Flustered, the night manager said he could, and the Detective and his partner crossed the room to talk to the waitress. She had curly dark hair and dark eyes and a quiet, attentive manner, like a naturalist, the Detective thought. Her attention was far away, for she didn't look up as the Detective and his partner approached. "Miss?"

"Excuse me," she said. "I was thinking about something." She glanced toward two tables, one occupied by an elderly couple, another by three men, one in his shirtsleeves, the other two still in jackets. "You're the police? You know I waited on the woman in 307?"

"Yes, we're the police," the Detective said. "And yeah, we heard you waited on Sally Johnson."

"She had the trout," she said. "Not that it matters."

"In some circumstances it might," the Detective said. "Did she eat alone?"

The waitress said, "She did."

"She expecting anyone?" the partner asked.

"She didn't ask to hold off her order. She didn't save a place."

"Did she watch people as they came in the place?"

"Not that I could see," the waitress answered.

"You had a lot of customers then?" the Detective asked.

"You kidding?" she said. "No one wants to work that hour, it's so slow. I had a few, some people who wanted tea, another group that wanted drinks only. The woman from 307. A man who ordered a whole fancy meal for himself, then hardly ate it. And this perfect family, husband, wife, two kids—not one thing looked wrong with them."

"Did she talk to anyone?"

"Not really," the waitress said. "The man with the family, he said something to her. As they were leaving, he stopped by the table and said something. She was eating the apple crumble and looked up a little startled. Then she laughed."

The partner asked, "And he was at…?"

"Table 11," she answered.

"And the loner?" the Detective asked.

"He was at Table 5."

She pointed out the large banquette the family had filled, the little round table where the loner had sat, and the deuce where Sally Johnson had been seated.

"How did they pay for their meals?" the Detective asked.

"The guy by himself," the waitress said, "he paid with a credit card. I'm pretty sure he wasn't staying here, which isn't unusual. They come for the food. I've heard it's good."

They thanked the waitress, then spent some time looking at Tables 5 and 11, draped with double tablecloths.

"You think a guy who pays with a credit card could be our guy?" the Detective asked.

"I think we should take prints down here," the partner said.

"That's crazy."

"Listen to me," the partner said. "All we have are dinner checks—dinner checks and our suspicions. And what good is that? If we found the same print down here that we found in the room, we'd be that much closer to linking our dinner guest with the credit card to the murder."

"Even if I didn't think that was cockamamie," the Detective said, "where are you going to find a print? On the table-cloths?"

"On the chair," the partner said.

"On the chair?"

The Detective spoke privately with the manager, then, his hands gloved, grasped the chair by the rear rung and moved it from Table 5 to a corner near the waitress. "As long as you're here, can you keep an eye on that for us?"

The waitress said yes.

The body had been bagged and removed by the time they returned to Room 307. The evidence technicians had stripped the blanket and top-sheet off the bed, so its expanse was exposed, as was the bloody pillow.

"Now that you're back, I can at last give you my preliminary report," the ME said dryly. "I hope you notice there is no bullet hole in the pillow."

"Just the victim's blood," the Detective said.

"Which means the cause of her death is still lodged in her brain." She paused to see that they were paying attention. "It pierced her skull enough to make her bleed, but not enough to exit." Because they were still listening, she continued.

"I estimate she died immediately after witnesses heard the gunshots, just before 6:55 p.m. You noticed the cadaveric spasm—the way she's holding her arm as if to protect herself? That posture of terror before death is an indicator that this was a homicide, not a suicide, and the victim died here. She was not moved."

"Well, all right then," the Detective said.

"It's not my place to add this," the ME said. "The pathologist determines this at the morgue, but I'd guess rape—both sides. But that's just my guess from looking at the body."

"Given the rest of the evidence," the Detective said, "we're not surprised. We'll be looking for the pathologist's confirmation." He added, "Sorry to have kept you from your other pressing engagements. We did have witnesses to interview."

"I know, I know," she said. "I just want to grab a smoke."

"You're excused," the Detective said.

"No she isn't," the partner said. "What about Desloratadine? What do you know about it?"

"Allergy medication?" the ME said. "That's all it is."

"Any side effects?" the partner asked.

"Drowsiness. Not suicide, that's for sure." She added, "Look, you're the ones who aren't excused. I need some information from you." She extracted her clipboard from her leather bag. "Like her name?"

When she left, tossing "See you next murder" over her shoulder, the evidence technicians shared a look the Detective didn't bother intercepting. He said, "What've you got?"

"A light show," one of the techs answered. The other switched on an ultraviolet light over the bed, semen stains fluorescing under it.

"So you will pack that up carefully?" the Detective asked.

"Always," the first tech answered. "The seminal fluid is already air-dried, but we always use paper bags. Last thing we want is mold on our bio samples. We're taking the pillow and the other bedding, too."

"The gun's secure?" the partner asked.

"First thing we did," the other tech said.

"It contained four live rounds and two spent casings," the first tech said, "and I labeled them carefully."

"We'll take that bullet with the plaster around it, so we don't damage the markings or any prints," the other tech said. "We already bagged the glasses, the bottle, and the ice bucket."

"Did you compare the ice-machine ice to what was in the bucket?" the Detective asked.

"We did," the first tech said. "Their machines make real one-inch-by-one-inch cubes with a characteristic concave side.

We're letting some melt in a plastic bucket, so we can take pictures of it as it melts."

"Good thinking," the Detective said.

"What kind of champagne was it?" the partner asked.

"We wrote it on the evidence label," the first tech said.

The Detective pulled the list from his pocket, then read the label: Piper-Heidsieck Champagne Brut. "It's not on our list."

"The bottle's got a store sticker on it," the first tech said. "A merchandise control sticker."

"So it's boosted," the partner said. "I guess he thought it was bring your own."

"And what immobile pieces are you going to dust?" the Detective asked, making sure that they planned to get finger-prints from the bureau, the nightstand, the knobs on both doors, the toilet, and the toilet seat, where men always leave excellent prints. "You did get a good sample of that urine in the bathroom?"

"We did that second," the first tech said.

"We're collecting very clean evidence."

"My partner and I want you to collect evidence in the restaurant, too," the Detective said, and then explained the prints he needed from the chair in the dining room.

"You think someone followed her up from the dining room?" the first tech asked.

"We think someone watched her in the dining room and snagged her room number when she charged the meal to the room."

"We think it could have been a Frankie Russo," the partner said. "This guy who sat at a table near hers."

"Or maybe this other guy who spoke to her," the Detective said.

Perhaps his partner shouldn't have used a name in front of the evidence technicians, but they were excited to think they had narrowed the field so quickly to two suspects simply by pulling from the dinner checks a credit card receipt for the lone diner at Table 5 and the signed check for the family at Table 11.

The following morning they attended the autopsy. The

pathologist confirmed the approximate time of death and agreed the manner was homicide, the mode was a gunshot from a .38-caliber revolver. She took an X-ray and showed them the way the bullet had pierced but not exited the back of Sally Johnson's skull.

"Given the abrasion and swelling and small tears, this was definitely a rape," the pathologist said. "Anal first, then vaginal, judging mostly by the body's position when you found her, but also by the disposition of the seminal fluid. It drained from her anus, but not from her vagina. We'll get very good DNA samples, by the way. You can compare them to that urine sample you told me about."

She pointed out faint pink bruises on the victim's shoulders. "Impressions of his eight fingers as he pressed her down to rape her from behind." She asked them to notice a pink mark beginning to darken "where he pressed her down with his strongest arm while he held the gun to her face." Before turning the victim, she removed the paper bags and checked the hands. "There was a struggle. I'm sure I have skin cells under her nails, if not blood." Because a gun was involved, the pathologist swabbed both hands with nitrous acid. "So you'll know if there was gunpowder on her hands. I mean, it seems like he controlled the gun, but you never can tell." When she turned the victim onto her back, the pathologist noted the matching bruises on the backs of the shoulders. "Where his palms and thumbs pressed. You can also see marks on her lower back, maybe when he first pressed her down on the bed, maybe when he held her down with one knee.

"He didn't beat her. He didn't pistol-whip her. I'm not sure why he killed her, unless killing is part of his thing. Did you put out a description of this crime to other police departments yet? Bet someone out there has a similar M.O."

The Detective tried calling the law firm that night, but chose not to leave a message asking them to call a detective in a distant city. So he called the next morning, and while on hold waiting to speak to the senior partner who was Sally Johnson's boss, the first fingerprint reports arrived in his inbox. He waved his partner over and showed him the results. One set of prints, presumed to be the suspect's, was found on the champagne bottle, the champagne glasses, and the ice bucket. The same prints were found on the bureau and nightstand, on the inside doorknob of Room 307, and on both bathroom doorknobs.

"And on the toilet seat," his partner said, "which at least he lifted."

"Habit," the Detective said.

There were two surprises, and the first was that they found only a partial from the suspect on the gun. They found a clear match for Sally Johnson.

"We didn't even consider it could be her gun," the Detective said. "We'd better trace the registration."

"We also didn't consider," the partner said, "that maybe they were fighting over the gun. Maybe she shot it."

"You think that first shot was hers?" the Detective asked.

"I do," the partner said. "I think she grabbed the gun while he was distracted. She tried to shoot, but he pushed her hand away, and that shot hit the wall."

"It was after that shot the witnesses said she really started screaming," the Detective said.

"Like he had control of the gun again."

"And she screamed until he shot her," the Detective said.

The second surprise was that though prints had been found on the restaurant chair and on the table-like surface above the banquette, none of them matched the prints in the room.

"It doesn't mean anything," the partner said.

"It means we have no reason to investigate either Russo or Clover."

Just then the senior partner came on the phone, and the Detective remembered he hadn't figured out yet what to say.

The Detective reported the crime to every police department in the state, but no one picked up on it. No one reported a similar modus operandi. He also submitted a report to the local FBI, so Sally Johnson's case could be entered in VICAP, the Violent Criminal Apprehension Program, and they could see if her murder could be linked to a known offender. The case did hit the news, and the tabloids immediately dubbed the suspect *The Champagne Rapist.* So while they waited for possible fingerprint matches from AFIS, while they checked to see if Sally Johnson had ever owned a registered gun, while they waited for the semen to be analyzed and the DNA fingerprints to be compared to the database, they sought help from the local FBI to sift through the VICAP database themselves. And they fielded a few calls from distant cities where similar crimes remained unsolved. The first call came from Vancouver, Washington, and the Detective and his partner both got on the phone and described what they believed happened.

"Somehow our guy spotted the victim and picked her out, probably while she ate dinner. We're pretty sure he found her room number after she signed off on her dinner check. We know he grabbed champagne glasses and an ice bucket from the hotel restaurant. But, he brought his own champagne, boosted from Shadytown Bridge Fine Wines and Liquor. He pulled a room-service ruse: 'You ordered champagne?' Something like that. He set down the champagne and the glasses, pulled his gun, and well, the rest you can paint without my help."

The Vancouver victim lived. She said the man knocked on her hotel door and said, "Someone ordered champagne for you." She said he didn't wear a mask or blindfold her, though he did sodomize her first, which she thought meant he was trying to hide. She submitted, because of the gun, but he smacked her near the end and threatened her life if she reported him.

That's the way it went. The Detective and his partner were wearing out their shoes talking to everyone on the lists they compiled, every employee in the Riverbank and the Shadytown Bridge Inn, every guest who had been registered that night. Some weeks later, while he was on the phone at his desk, the Detective looked down at the list hotel security had drawn up that night. It was the list the uniformed officer had requested, the one she'd used to go room to room in the hotel, canvassing all the guests. That night, after the evidence technicians had cleared out and he had locked the door behind him and discussed with security the precautions they should take as long as the room remained a crime scene, he sat in the lobby with the officer, going over her meticulous notes and thanking her for her good work. As he did so, he leaned back in his chair, put his hands behind his head, and realized what a clear view one could have of the dining room. It must have been someone's intention, to let the passersby see the white tables, the dimly glowing walls.

At his desk, the Detective looked at the list of hotel guests and understood that his guy could have watched Sally Johnson from all sorts of places in that lobby—even that chair where he'd sat taking pressure off his knee. He remembered the man sitting next to him, while his partner parked the car and he waited for hotel security. He'd walked across the lobby, past the people lined up to check out, and sat down next to the Detective, setting a paper bag at his feet—an elegant bag with raffia handles: Shadytown Bridge Fine Wines and Liquor. After a few minutes, he'd gotten up and taken the next taxi.

Bibliography

1. Thomas F. Adams, Alan G. Caddell, and Jeffrey L. Krutsinger, *Crime Scene Investigation*, Prentice Hall, 2004. [A paperback book written by crime scene investigators that focuses on basic crime scene investigation procedures.]

2. Dr. Michael Baden, M.D., and Marion Roach, *Death Reckoning—The New Science of Catching Killers*, Simon and Schuster, 2001. [This book focuses on dead bodies and related evidence examined in death investigations. It is based on Dr. Baden's 40-year career in forensic pathology, during which he conducted more than 20,000 autopsies.]

3. Colin Evans, *The CASEBOOK of Forensic Detection—How Science Solved 100 of the World's Most Baffling Crimes*, John Wiley & Sons, Inc., 1996. [A chronology of 100 international criminal cases broken down in categories of the types of forensic evidence and analyses used to solve them.]

4. Barry A. J. Fisher, *Techniques of Crime Scene Investigation*, CRC Press, 2000. [More of a handbook or how-to book for practitioners and students that includes field-tested techniques and procedures, plus technical information.]

5. David Fisher, *HARD EVIDENCE—How Detectives Inside the FBI's Sci-Crime Lab Have Helped Solve America's Toughest Cases*, Dell Publishing, 1995. [A paperback book on the FBI's

crime laboratory and how investigators inside the lab have helped solve America's toughest criminal cases.]

6. Vernon J. Geberth, *Practical Homicide Investigation— Tactics, Procedures, and Forensic Techniques*, CRC Press, 1993. [Based on the author's 25 years of experience as a New York City detective and homicide commander, his book is a comprehensive treatise that deals with every aspect of death investigation.]

7. John Houde, *CRIME LAB: A Guide for Nonscientists*, Calico Press, 1999. [Describes each step of the analysis of evidence gathered at crime scenes, including 130 illustrations that explain in easy-to-understand concepts exactly what's happening along the way.]

8. Keith Inman and Norah Rudin, *Principles and Practice of Criminalistics—The Profession of Forensic Science*, CRC Press, 2001. [Presents a timeline of the history and evolution of criminalistics, and the principles and practice of forensic science.]

9. Dr. Henry C. Lee, *CRACKING CASES—The Science of Solving Crimes*, Prometheus Books, 2002. [An analysis of the entire investigative process of five murder cases, including Sherman, MacArthur, O. J. Simpson, Mathison, and Woodchipper.]

10. Thomas P. Mauriello, *Criminal Investigation Handbook— Strategy, Law and Science*, Matthew Bender & Company, Inc., Edition # 13, 2003. [The "bible" of treatises on the subject of criminal investigation that is never out-of-date. First published in 1990, this treatise is revised each year, ensuring that the information presented is always current and accurate.]

11. Robert R. Ogle, Jr., *Crime Scene Investigation and Reconstruction*, Prentice Hall, 2004. [A textbook for both practitioners and students of crime scene investigation.]

12. Richard Saferstein, *Criminalistics—An Introduction to Forensic Science*, Eighth Edition, Prentice Hall, 2004. [Presented as the standard for forensic science procedures during the O.J. Simpson trial by the defense, this is a technical book for crime laboratory scientist or physical science students. The focus is on laboratory analysis and procedures.]

13. Jessica Snyder Sachs, *Corpse—Nature, Forensics, and the Struggle to Pinpoint Time of Death*, Perseus Publishing, 2001. [This book identifies all the forensic sciences used to attempt to pinpoint time of death. A first of its kind, this book is a must-read for anyone learning about the clues of the post-mortem body.]

14. Timothy Sweetman and Adele Sweetman, *Investigating a Homicide*, Copperhouse Publishing Company, 1997. [A workbook designed for academic use to accommodate a semester of weekly in-class homicide investigation cases.]

15. Judy Williams, *The Modern Sherlock Holmes—An Introduction to Forensic Science Today*, Broadside Books, 1991. [A well-written and illustrated book that brings up-to-date forensic science methods set down by Sherlock Holmes. The text focuses on work done in England in this regard.]